CONTEXTUAL THEOLOGY

Intersectionality of Gender, Race, and Class

HiRho Y. Park, PhD, and Cynthia A. Bond Hopson, PhD, General Editors

HIGHER EDUCATION & MINISTRY
General Board of Higher Education and Ministry
THE UNITED METHODIST CHURCH

Contextual Theology: Intersectionality of Gender, Race, and Class

The General Board of Higher Education and Ministry leads and serves The United Methodist Church in the recruitment, preparation, nurture, education, and support of Christian leaders—lay and clergy—for the work of making disciples of Jesus Christ for the transformation of the world. Its vision is that a new generation of Christian leaders will commit boldly to Jesus Christ and be characterized by intellectual excellence, moral integrity, spiritual courage, and holiness of heart and life. The General Board of Higher Education and Ministry of The United Methodist Church serves as an advocate for the intellectual life of the church. The Board's mission embodies the Wesleyan tradition of commitment to the education of laypersons and ordained persons by providing access to higher education for all persons.

Contextual Theology: Intersectionality of Gender, Race, and Class

ISBN 978-1-945935-79-4

GBHEM Publishing is an affiliate member of the Association of University Presses.

Manufactured in the United States of America

HIGHER EDUCATION & MINISTRY
General Board of Higher Education and Ministry
THE UNITED METHODIST CHURCH

Contents

iii

CONTENTS

Introduction

HiRho Y. Park, PhD

In August 2019, twelve Methodist African and Asian women theologians gathered for a seminar in Seoul, Korea, sponsored by the General Board of Higher Education and Ministry (GBHEM) of The United Methodist Church. Dr. Beauty Maenzanise, who served as dean of Africa University School of Theology in Zimbabwe, gave leadership to invite women theologians from Africa. I, as an Asian American woman, worked with Dr. Hyun Ju Lee and Dr. Yani Yoo, who teach at Methodist Theological University in South Korea, to invite women theologians from Asia. Dr. Kathy Armistead, publisher of GBHEM, gave leadership by encouraging African and Asian women theologians to publish their work. This book is a collection of theological writings from those who participated in the African and Asian Methodist Women Theologians' Seminar. It was a prophetic event because the voice of African and Asian women theologians is often muted in academia, and it is a challenge to publish their academic work due to the presumption of incompetency of racial-ethnic women, which is exacerbated by the idea that their approaches to theological work are not legitimate for the standard of the Western male-oriented academy. Their theological work is often pigeonholed even in their own countries as a liberal feminist agenda because of their national needs of survival and liberation. I hope that this book will provide grounds to take African and Asian women's theological work seriously beyond the politics of representation.

During the seminar, twelve African and Asian women theologians exchanged ideas on the subject of the intersectionality of gender, race, class, and theology. The goals of the seminar were to celebrate African and Asian women's theological work and share theological heritage and uniqueness from the two regions. These women brought multireligious and diverse cultural and political experiences that can serve to reconstruct theology, making it more contextual and more relevant. Both African and Asian women are situated within the nexuses of patriarchy, colonialism, and Western imperialism; they include their experiences of colonialism and victimization in their countries as essential components of theological construction. Their theologies are born out of the contexts of plurality; they are seeking to be seen as fully human in a political, economic, cultural, and religious sense. Their theological work integrates women's heritage in African and Asian culture and history that may be found in Shamanism, Confucianism, and Christianity to provide a foundation for value, dignity, and power for women.

John Wesley, the founder of Methodism, considered human experience essential for keeping theology a practical discipline. African and Asian women's theologies require sharing their experiences as a way to voice their discrete cultural ideas related to their self-understandings of Christian wisdom (*phronesis*).[1] Christian wisdom contains within it the practical reason of a faith community that is based on symbols and convictions, which provide a firm foundation for practical theology. This book is meant to be a "theological reorientation," as delineated by Andrea Smith in her article "Dismantling the Master's House with the Master's Tools: Native Feminist Liberation Theologies."[2] Theological reorientation allows discourse about faith and God to be fluent and flexible as it is interpreted according to one's own context. For example, Musimbi R. A. Kanyoro argues that the real challenge for African women theologians is not about theologizing what justice for women is; it is rather about bringing changes into practice. She explains that because women in Africa are guardians of culture and tradition, it is challenging to bring changes connecting Church, home, and society.

Rita Nakashima Brock, a Japanese-American theologian, also asserts that Caucasian feminist theology is inadequate to address the racism, colonialism, and economic exploitation—in addition to sexism—that Asian women have experienced.[3] The African and Asian women authors in this book use a method of

---

1 Don S. Browning, *A Fundamental Practical Theology* (Minneapolis: Fortress Press, 1996), 10.

2 Andrea Smith, "Dismantling the Master's House with the Master's Tools: Native Feminist Liberation Theologies" in *Hope Abundant: Third World and Indigenous Women's Theology*, ed. Kwok Pui-Lan (Maryknoll, NY: Orbis Books, 2010), 76.

3 Rita Nakashima Brock, "Cooking without Recipes: Interstitial Integrity," in *Off the Menu: Asian and Asian North American Women's Religion and Theology*, ed. Rita Nakashima Brock et al. (Louisville: Westminster John Knox Press, 2007), 126.

"indigenous theory"[4] to recover the image of God that was lost among women due to historical and cultural oppression in their countries.

African and Asian women share unique theological commonalities even though they are from totally different areas in the world. First, their theologies are relational. Second, patriarchy (male dominance) is a key subject of doing theology. Third, decolonizing interpretation of the Bible against the cultural hegemony of the West is the foundation of their theological self-determination.

Relational Theology

According to Wonhee Anne Joh, the human community is "constituted in and through relationality with all others."[5] The core claim of African and Asian women's theologies is that women's liberation is a part of the liberation of all people, including all oppressors; an individual can never be separated from a community, regardless of his or her gender. Solidarity of the community is the foundation of all relationality in both cultures; an individual's faithfulness is closely related to her community and what it means to be a faithful church.[6] Therefore, the struggle for the emancipation

---

4   Gayatri Chakravorty Spivak, *The Postcolonial Critic: Interviews, Strategies, Dialogues,* ed. Sarah Harasym (New York: Routledge, 1990), 69. Spivak asserts that one can construct an indigenous theory when she reflects on the history from her own perspective.

5   Wonhee Anne Joh, "Violence and Asian American Experience: From Abjection to Jeong," in *Off the Menu,* ed. Rita N. Brock et al., 146–47.

6   Musimbi R. A. Kanyoro, "Engendered Communal Theology: African Women's Contribution to Theology in the Twenty-First Century," in *Hope Abundant,* ed. Kwok, 20.

of women should be a communal praxis. Choi Hee An coined the phrase "a postcolonial self" to recognize a community-oriented construction of theology. "A postcolonial self" is a communal self, and it only thrives when one coexists with "I and we with others."[7] This community-oriented construction of theology is very different than Western theology, which is rooted in individualism. In doing theology, both African and Asian women consider carefully the importance of balance and wholeness of the human community, which begins at home and extends to the community, society, nation, and world. African and Asian women theologians seek harmony with other human beings and nature. They value the feminine role in relating to a community—such as being a mother, caring for the family, and respecting mutuality in relationship with others—as assets to constructing theology.

Patriarchy, the Key Subject

Gender equality is still a challenge in Africa and Asia. Gayatri Chakravorty Spivak once said that "even the most disenfranchised man has more rights within a patriarchal society."[8] African and Asian women have been struggling against the traditional cultural female virtues of self-sacrifice, obedience, and subservience. They have been dealing with the double tasks of challenging androcentric myths in Christianity and confronting patriarchal practices in their culture and society. Doing theology means deconstructing existing traditional interpretations of the Bible by incorporating political and cultural women's experiences

---

7   Choi Hee An, *A Postcolonial Self: Korean Immigrant Theology and Church* (Albany, NY: SUNY Press, 2015).

8   Spivak, *The Postcolonial Critic*, 139.

systematically. They share a resistance to patriarchy in their theological discourse because patriarchy is the logic that naturalizes social hierarchy and a heteronormative gender binary system.[9] As a response to the multifaceted women's issues in a global context, Elisabeth Schüssler Fiorenza proposes shifting the focus of cultural biases against women from patriarchy to kyriarchy because the latter addresses more comprehensive and multiplicative forms of oppression.[10]

Kyriarchy operates under an imperialistic mode of maintaining power and control over the powerless in all aspects of life. Schüssler Fiorenza starts her argument by asserting that the role of patriarchy only grants structural and institutional relations of male domination. Therefore, Schüssler Fiorenza proposes to use kyriarchy to articulate the complexity of oppressive structures and power struggles among women. Kyriarchy incorporates the multilayered interdependence of gender, race, and class stratifications in social systems that consist of patriarchy, ideology, and capitalism. As an ideology, kyriocentrism sets roadblocks against women based on linguistic, cultural, ideological, and institutional differences.[11] African and Asian women articulate kyriocentrism that prevents their theological engagement from being subjective agents in their writings.

---

9   Smith, "Dismantling the Master's House," 81.

10 The word *kyriarchy* is derived from "the Greek words for 'lord' or 'master' (*kyrios*) and 'to rule or dominate' (*archein*), which seeks to redefine the analytic category of patriarchy in terms of multiplicative intersecting structures of domination." Kyriarchy is a complex pyramidal system of domination that works through the violence of economic exploitation and lived subordination. Schüssler Fiorenza, *Wisdom Ways: Introducing Feminist Biblical Interpretation* (Maryknoll, NY: Orbis Books, 2001), 211.

11 Fiorenza, 124.

Decolonizing Theological Interpretation

African and Asian women theologians challenge the theological imperialism of the West by insisting that their particular experiences provide validity of theological self-determination. They theologize their experiences from a site of emancipation, which requires an interdisciplinary methodology. The subversive character of their theology is a result of interpreting the Scripture from spiritual, social, cultural, economic, and gender perspectives, based on their life experiences. For example, Musa W. Dube calls the Bible "imperialist text" and argues that Western binary and hierarchical interpretation of the Bible furthered African women's subjugation in the Church and society. She says, "To read the Bible as an African is to take a perilous journey, a sinister journey that spins one back to connect with dangerous memories of slavery, colonialism, apartheid, and neo-colonialism."[12]

The Church indeed provided women with an emancipatory space in Africa and Asia, where they once were bound in a domestic realm. However, African and Asian women still find the Church to be a gendered and racialized institution where the dominant Western capitalism and imperialistic theological interpretation dictate women's leadership. African and Asian women theologians point out the global theological trend of neo-colonial impulses by urging not to continue postcolonial hierarchy between the West and the rest of the world. The postcolonial hierarchy expands when the Bible is interpreted, justifying lesser humanity of those who are living in the periphery of life, including women and the marginalized.

---

12 Musa W. Dube, "Toward a Postcolonial Feminist Interpretation of the Bible," in *Hope Abundant*, ed. Kwok, 90-91.

Now, we will take a journey with some African and Asian women as they articulate their theologies. I hope readers will let these women speak for themselves from their subjective, cultural, historical, and institutional positions. I hope these writings will be a starting point for affirming African and Asian women's ability to claim their own subjectivity, attesting women's ability to articulate their feelings of indignation and evoking a theology of suspicion among African and Asian women. The spirit of these women theologians may inspire younger African and Asian women in the overall understanding of an oppressive reality, empowering them to acknowledge themselves as human beings who are entitled to social, political, cultural, economic, educational, and religious access.

Cynthia A. Bond Hopson, an African American journalism excellence scholar, declares the socially constructed intersections of race and gender collide when pitted against each other. She joins forces with these learned theologians to raise her voice with authenticity and authority on how overcoming stereotypes of women of color, their invisibility, and how coupling the scourge of poverty and class warfare with race and gender intersections make thriving and surviving a daily challenge. Bond Hopson shares poignant examples of why her career as an academician, higher-education executive, writer, professor, and truth teller are a perfect complement to views contained here. Her *just-the-facts* storytelling invites readers to add context for a fuller picture of why intersections must matter.

Djessou Epse Atsin Djoman Brigitte from Côte d'Ivoire expounds on how women can transform society and contribute to human liberation in a deteriorating male-dominant society. She says, "Under the heavyweight of economic crises with wars with their procession of refugees and violence that continues to shake

Africa, the family model built on the primacy of male power is cracking, decaying, and exposing increasingly unbearable contradictions from the point of equity, of justice." This changing socioeconomic situation demands that gender relations must evolve. She asserts that women are "creating a culture of peace" in Côte d'Ivoire, and creating peace can only be achieved through a partnership with women. She states that our humanity is portrayed in roots that speak to our relationality. Djoman Brigitte reviews strategies of biblical women for them to share their responsibilities of leading transformation as a methodology.

Elaine Wei-Fun Goh from Malaysia examines how the interpretation of Ecclesiastes 7:23-8:1 bolstered four main Chinese cultural admonitions of women—describing women as a "Lady Folly" whose wickedness may trap a man who seeks wisdom. The traditional interpretation of these verses reinforced that women should pursue the ideal Chinese cultural image of a virtuous, soft-spoken, meek, and prudent worker. Otherwise, she is a Lady Folly, dangerous inside and out, which contributed to creating a gendered church and society. Goh suggests that one must guard one's cultural biases when reading biblical texts and offers an alternative reading to the Ecclesiastes passage.

Helena Angelica Gustavo Guidione explores how the Bible has enabled the patriarchal oppression of women in Southern Mozambique. The androcentric interpretation of the Bible makes it difficult for women to participate in ministry as leaders, even though they have made great strides in the political arena as governors, ministers, and administrators. However, Mozambican women are still pursuing a seat at the table to make critical decisions, and a new way of interpreting the Bible can advance practical change in the Church and society.

Hyun Ju Lee examines Western white male dominance in the early twentieth-century mission field using the theory of intersectionality of race, gender, and class. To make her case, she investigates two Korean novels: *Ewa: A Tale of Korea* (1906), written by William Arthur Noble, an American male missionary, and *Daybreak in Korea* (1909), a novel written by Annie Laurie Baird, an American female missionary. Lee identifies evidence of eschewed portraits of Korean women as nonintellectual, domestic sexual objects based on patriarchy and Western imperialism.

Memory Chikosi laments how local churches reflect patriarchal Zimbabwean society rather than God's intended future for the community of faith. Chikosi asserts that women and men are meant to be mutually interrelated. She examines gender inequality by analyzing theological education in seminaries, which aggravates the continuation of women's exploitation. She urges a need for revision of curriculum in theological schools and calls the Church to lead the way to gender equality.

Quynh-Hoa Nguyen charges the Church for the way it has contributed to reinforcing patriarchy that justifies the power relation of dominance and submission of women in Vietnamese society. Nguyen interprets the household codes (Ephesians 5-6, Colossians 3, and 1 Peter 3) from a new perspective; she indicates that one of the barriers is that the Bible teaches male domination and female subordination. The patriarchal biblical interpretation engenders submission, marginalization, and exclusion of the weak and powerless. As an alternative, she suggests a partnership between male and female that transgresses the traditional male-dominated structures toward support, submission, respect, acknowledgment, and empowerment. She uses the image of chopsticks to explain a metaphor symbolizing a power balance and mutuality.

Yani Yoo examines how Judges 21, a story of the collective abduction of women and forced marriages; a Korean folk story, "The Fairy and the Woodcutter"; and the recent sexual criminal case of the Burning Sun Club in Seoul, Korea are interrelated in terms of taking, controlling, and exploiting women's bodies for profit. She argues that all of these stories take women's bodies for the economic interests of men, while the voices of women are muted. Instead, women in these stories suffer from self-condemnation and judgment. She disputes that women's lives serve men's economic, sexual, social, and cultural interests in the Church and society.

HiRho Y. Park claims that institutional tokenism is a new form of racism that stems out of egalitarian intellectual romanticism in academia and the Church. She portrays how token racial-ethnic women in the U.S. struggle with triple burdens: how they perform as women, how they represent their racial-ethnic category, and how they carry traditional and cultural role-play as daughters, wives, and mothers. Yet she seeks a way forward from being a token as a God-given opportunity to lead. Thriving within a place of microaggressions is only possible when a token is aware of being a token, and this is a special calling from God. Park also argues that fighting against institutional tokenism should be a communal task by creating a supportive network among token racial-ethnic women.

ONE

Becoming a Whole from the Sum of Parts

Race, Class, and Gender Intersections and Transformations

CYNTHIA A. BOND HOPSON, PHD

Scholarly African American women, like other women and women of color, grapple daily with dualities in their existence. First, the question is, Can we be taken seriously as authentic and authoritative voices on substantive social matters and critical academic challenges; or must we be measured by race and gender, both vying for prime position, and never measuring up?

For the scope of this work, the question becomes, Is the totality of African American women scholars greater than a sum of their impressive parts? The easy answer is yes, but reality is much more complicated. We must decide, Can these smart, successful women get past the noise and distortions of stereotypes, warped expectations, and a society hell-bent on defining and distracting them, or not?

In our world we are often influenced by media and images they generate, both positive and negative. The pictures, inuendoes, and illustrations are powerful; and they help us decide who and what is important. When the intersections of race, class, and gender are factored into the same equation, it is easy to ignore that these pieces are nonnegotiable and equal.

According to Dates and Barlow, in their classic *Split Image: African Americans in the Mass Media*,[1] "the mass media help to legitimate the inequalities in class and race relations." The editors purport that racial images in the mass media are moralistically color coded positive and negative, and when used often enough, these mind pictures "fuel imperceptions and perpetuate misunderstandings among the races." Couple these problematic images with conversations about African American women, and a scenario for inequality, stress, and disenfranchisement emerges.

On Being Invisible and Taking Turns

I purposely wore red that Wednesday afternoon. Researchers have shown that dressing professionally, and especially wearing red, helps establish credibility and makes presenters seem more knowledgeable and confident in their subject matter.[2]

As the only African American member of Murray State University's journalism/radio/TV faculty, I loved doing guest diversity lectures. I was starving, so I allowed time for lunch before

---

1   Jannette L. Dates and William Barlow, eds., *Split Image: African Americans in the Mass Media* (Washington, D.C.: Howard University Press, 1990), 4-5.

2   Mohammad Abul Kashem, "The Effect of Teachers' Dress on Students' Attitude and Students' Learning: Higher Education View," *Education Research International* 2019, Article ID 9010589 (Dec 26, 2019), https://doi.org/10.1155/2019/9010589.

my presentation and was feeling confident and well prepared when I entered the right side of the Pizza Hut, across from the left door.

I stood near the "Please wait to be seated" sign and watched servers and hosts scurry back and forth with their orders and duties. About three minutes in I wondered if I had been rendered invisible, because nobody asked if I had been served or needed some help.

This was the first time wearing red had not gotten me noticed. I was looking accomplished and competent but was still being ignored. After about five minutes the door on the left opened, and a Bradley Cooper-looking man came in and was immediately surrounded by servers and greeters. He smiled as the host asked him, "Smoking or non?"

I stood there, with smoke coming out of my nose and mouth by this time, still with no acknowledgment from any of the restaurant's staff. What happened next still amazes me. The gentleman they had flocked to said, "She was here first." The host immediately turned to me, said she had not seen me waiting, and asked, "Smoking or non?"

I was so angry at having endured what many women and people of color endure every day—invisibility, insensitivity, harassment, and/or benign neglect—and even recalling the experience now makes me angry all over again. I thanked the young man and said, "That's never happened before."

"But it wasn't my turn," he said shyly.

Something as small as waiting for your turn, "seeing," and acknowledging others makes a world of difference. Seeing difference is equally critical and being tolerant and appreciative of it is even more important. Asking questions for clarity and fairness, being sensitive, seeing the totality of individuals instead of lumping individuals with their group, are all pieces of the same giant puzzle that poignantly reminds us that intersections matter. Whether on highways, on city streets, in boardrooms, in the academy, or at synagogue or church, intersections matter; and the whole is far greater than the sum of its parts.

Oftentimes stereotypes of women and people of color are subconsciously internalized, and the frustration and hurt that results manifests itself with violence or bad attitudes at the slightest inclination or provocation. For example, the loaded language depicted in Westerns and Native American uprisings makes it seem that the settlers were viciously attacked for no reason. Further, when the British and others invaded African countries, and tribesmen turned them back or defended their land and way of life, words like *savages* and *massacre* were used to describe what transpired. Unfortunately, historical accounts with words like *massacre* and *savagely killed* omit contextual clues that would make the defensive actions make sense. Native Americans and Africans simply defended themselves from the invaders.

Rarely is a cause/effect rationale offered to defend or dispel myths about why African American women, no matter their economic status, oftentimes suffer poor health, seem angry or difficult, or lash out. Usually their reactions are not isolated but come after repeated instances of dismissal, harassment, or being rendered invisible or insignificant. Much like the afternoon before the diversity lecture, I was expecting to have a positive experience imparting knowledge and discussing an important topic.

For the record, from my research, African American women do not get up every morning and drink a can of "whoop___" for breakfast; yet when we defend ourselves, we often get labeled "difficult" or "too sensitive."

The week before my visit to Pizza Hut, I was next in line at a local boutique, when the Caucasian clerk returned from the back and asked the young Caucasian woman behind me if she needed help. When the young woman stepped up to take my turn, I politely said, "I was here first." The clerk said, "I didn't know who was first." "Always ask if you don't know" was my reply. The young woman behind me knew whose turn it was but opted to take the privilege and a turn she had not earned. The clerk burst into tears though I didn't yell, scream, get loud, use profanity, or "do the neck thing."[3] I simply said, "I was here first."

Living through the white privilege exhibited by the clerk and the customer behind me are all in a day's work. White privilege, according to the *Washington Post*, "is a societal advantage that comes with being seen as the norm in America, and it is automatically conferred irrespective of wealth, gender or other factors." This *advantage* usually eases the way for whites at the expense of others, though many whites don't know it is there or deny its existence or their role in perpetuating it.[4]

Most days being first is not a deal breaker. It is about fairness; it is a matter of justice, of speaking for one's self, a matter of self-determination. In March 1827 when *Freedom's Journal*, the nation's first African American newspaper, was started, John B. Russwurm and Samuel Cornish said the motivation was to

---

3   The neck thing is an action on the path to anger and outrage, which includes rolling the head and neck, and heated and matter-of-fact explanations.

4   Christine Emba, "What Is White Privilege?" *The Washington Post*, January 16, 2016, www.washingtonpost.com/blogs/post-partisan/wp /2016/01/16/white-privilege-explained/.

plead their own case, for "far too long have others spoken for us." With pressing issues facing individuals, families, academicians, communities, and organizations, African American women in the academy must stay alert and vigilant. Though they must be careful to not start fights, when they find themselves in one, they must fight like hell for their womanhood, for their right to be taken seriously, to be secure in their racial identity, and for the equity, dignity, and equality they deserve. Race, class, and gender variables are equal to and greater than their individual parts in much the same way that hands and feet and eyes and ears complement each other.

Race, class, and gender issues continue to be downplayed until the surface is scratched, even lightly.

African American Women Scholars: Finding Our Way

As public intellectuals, scholars, academicians, and Christians, many of us were taught from the beginning to love ourselves and our neighbors, to respect the rights of others, to follow Micah 6:8 and do justice, love mercy, and walk humbly with God. Rarely was there explicit information given about the evolving, paradoxical, and societal changes that would eventually affect us and the decisions we get to make.

Race and gender are nonnegotiable entities, but class is more difficult to navigate. It is aspirational for those who strive to change their lot and status. Who we become, where we live, who we marry, and how we choose to live our dailiness has evolved; and going forward, race, class, and gender as social constructs will dictate and offer societal challenges, create uncomfortable paradoxes, and prompt changing definitions about ourselves and how we get along in society.

An example of the shifting ground we stand on came during preparation for the 2020 United States Census, as controversy arose over "race" options participants could choose. Choosing one box for multiracial persons was problematic, and there were advocates and opponents alike. Further, over the past decade, states and government entities have grappled with what eventually became known as "bathroom laws," or privileges and provisions for transgendered or people who were born with a gender classification they no longer live in. For the first time in an election cycle, there was an openly gay competitive presidential candidate. Television and movie ads are now peppered with interracial, biracial, and gay couples as marriage laws changed to allow same-sex marriages and adoptions.

New, restrictive laws were enacted or threatened, and boycotts and toilet seat protests on the front lawns of legislative facilities proved effective in continuing the conversation around gender and its fluid nature. During 2020's COVID-19 global pandemic, more than thirty million claims were filed for unemployment insurance in a two-month period during a virtual shutdown of the business and governmental sectors, and a barrage of media coverage highlighted how fragile most people's personal finances are.

Personal wealth suffered from a weak stock market and a global economy that could not sustain itself. Bankruptcies and business closings abounded, and the miles-long lines for food assistance brought many US cities to a place not seen since the Great Depression.

Class is a touchy subject and one most people don't wander into without fair warning. As a matter of fact, "the word 'class' is fraught with unpleasant associations, so that to linger upon it is apt to be interpreted as the symptom of a perverted spirit."[5] In recent elections the topic of "two Americas, one rich and one poor" sparked interest but not much change, and very few efforts have served to lift those in the lower classes to a comfortable middle-class rung.

In conversations around stimulus funds for COVID-19 displaced workers and closed businesses, efforts by legislators were designed to make sure small businesses and individuals received the funds and not big, rich corporations. Talking about class makes many people uncomfortable no matter where they fall on the spectrum.

Poverty is big business, and many people get and stay wealthy because of it. Whether it's exploitation of the poor, attitudes about who is poor and their worth, or laws enacted to provide help to the rich in the form of tax breaks, incentives, or special projects, the poor keep getting poorer while the rich get richer, according to economists. African Americans have traditionally not been able to depend on generational wealth but have found that education is the great equalizer for those who want to aspire and move forward.

According to Dr. Dorothy Granberry, in a discussion of the four professional African American women chronicled in *The Women of Haywood: Their Lives, Our Legacy,* an oral history collection:

> Attainment of education and holding a position that paid a salary or produced a predictable income changed these women's economic conditions—made them more independent, allowed them greater maneuvering room, and made it possible for them to be more broadly exposed to evolving ideas and practices. This confluence of factors

5   Paul Fussell, *Class: A Guide Through the American Status System* (New York: Touchstone Publishers, 1992), 15.

made them vehicles for change in that they are knowledge-able, caring, responsible, can see ahead, believe in team-work, and they sing no victim's song.[6]

Education = Middle-Class Privilege = Living the American Dream, Moving on Up?

Ariel was one of my favorite students, though I had worked hard not to show favoritism and treat them all the same. When he was missing from class, I called. He was sick, and the next thing I knew he was hospitalized. My two-and-a-half-hour commute prevented me from immediately going to see him, but I was stunned when he said he was there at the hospital by himself. Where in the world were his parents? He said they were about the same distance from him as I was, and they could not come.

I went through the "if my child were sick" scenarios and got busy connecting him to my United Methodist network. When I got back to Memphis, he was still in the hospital, but his father had arrived. His father humbly explained that he worked for one of the major car companies, and if he doesn't work the day before and after the holiday, he doesn't get the specialty pay. I felt an inch tall, because I had not even considered the economy of taking off work for a sick child nor had I had to because I have earned a salary for the past thirty-five years.

Privilege of the middle class and the luxury of being able to work nine months and study or rebuild my skills during the sum-mer are all class perks; and while I have not always been a scholar and gentlewoman, there are many things we take for granted.

---

6   Cynthia Bond Hopson, ed., *The Women of Haywood: Their Lives, Our Legacy* (Lebanon, TN: Touched by Grace Publications, 2012), 48–49.

Like bank accounts that allow access to your funds without paying to get checks cashed. Like earning a decent wage that allows for timely bill payment and great rates on loans to keep you from being at the mercy of payday lenders and title loan sharks.

Class differences raise their ugly heads during natural disasters and pandemics as the poor bear a disproportionate amount of displacement, disruption, death, and destruction. In major cities, with high rents and a shortage of affordable housing, the homeless get rounded up and hidden during big tourist events. During the winter the shelters are filled past capacity because of the vast abundance of homeless, whose numbers have increased dramatically due to poor mental health support, a tumultuous economy, and the glaring but usually overlooked common denominator, access to a good education.

Many middle-class parents sacrifice to send their children to prestigious private schools for the accelerated curriculum but also for the social capital their children get from their well-to-do peers. Children from poor or lower-middle class families, mostly first-generation students who populate many of the nation's Historically Black Colleges and Universities (HBCU), greatly improve their lot by graduating or even spending one year in college.

During race, class, and gender discussions in my writing and editing classes, some students would become irate because we were having the conversation. One adult learner shouted: "I'm sick and tired of talking about diversity. Why do we have to talk about it all the time?" I asked if she lived in a perfect world. She said no. I asked if everyone she knew had a decent place to eat, sleep, and relax. Again, she said no.

"When we have a perfect world and everyone has what they need when they need it, then we can stop talking about it," was my terse reply.

If I Were You, I'd Ride the Black Woman Thing for All It's Worth—Race and Gender: Intersection or Head-On Collision

As an African American scholar and thought leader, I deliberately integrate the intersections of race, class, and gender in every phase of my work. I could not separate my race from my gender from my class if someone gave out rewards for the best disengagement. That's why I was taken aback by the recruiter's advice.

I wandered over to the student center where the graduate fair was being held and stopped at the table of one of the big majority-serving schools. He asked if I had chosen a school, then he said almost as an afterthought, "If I were you, I'd ride that Black and woman thing for all it's worth. You're a 'twofer,' and schools love it when they get two for the price of one." I assured him I don't know how to be anything other than an African American woman. I live with having to prove my worth daily, with being followed in stores while I shop, and/or with being hired for a job without any duties. Every day I live with having to be proficient enough to walk with kings but humble enough to eat with peasants. I did not need his inane advice.

The accomplished and capable African American woman standing in front of him had "lived, worked, and struggled under disparate and often contradictory social circumstances"[7] as *Black Feminist Thought* author Patricia Hill Collins put it and lived to triumphantly tell the story. God created the intersections to bless our lives so we can count it all joy!

---

7   Angela Y. Davis, back cover endorsement for Patricia Hill Collins, *Fighting Words: Black Women and the Search for Justice* (Minneapolis: University of Minnesota Press, 1998).

TWO

The Liberation of Humanity

Lessons from History and
New Testament Women

DJESSOU EPSE ATSIN DJOMAN BRIGITTE, PhD

In some societies, women have long been subjected to abuse. Women have even been merely considered property that could be passed along as part of men's inheritance. Yet, on that Resurrection Sunday morning, the Gospels agree that a woman was chosen as worthy to proclaim the message of eternal life. This single event is of paramount importance, because it demonstrates that women can be indispensable and responsible members of society with a rightful place—that they are free agents and capable of leadership to help transform the world and align it with the kingdom of God. To this end, women, as givers of life and chosen by God to bear the good news, must commit to the transformation of society in order to free all humanity, both men and women.

The purpose of this chapter is to discuss social transformation and human liberation by looking through a theological lens to examine how New Testament women acted to transform their context and liberate their people. It also will take into account the history of the Church as rooted in African traditions. This chapter rests on the conviction that women's struggle for equal opportunity is the precious foundation for a just, peaceful, viable society that will benefit all of us.

But even in African countries today, we should note that power is held largely by men. Human dignity seems to have disappeared; people are suffering and living in poverty; men and women are subjected to physical, moral, and spiritual death. One only must follow the world's media reports to see the state of our male-owned societies. Why? one may ask. It may well be simply because of the patriarchal approach to power that is amplified by the willingness of some men to exclude women from positions of influence where they might make other decisions. However, let us remember that women are the source of life and the first educator of children, both male and female. Because of women, children are nurtured and take their first steps to reach their intellectual and spiritual potential. It was the same in biblical times; therefore it might be helpful and informative to seek exemplars of women from the Bible and Church history.

Throughout the Church, women, with a thirst for justice, have mobilized in a quest for freedom and equality. We see this in their rejection of patriarchal oppression by opening new spaces for expressions and by redefining partnerships between men and women. In order to change outcomes, old paradigms must be broken, because society cannot establish new priorities without eliminating inequality between women and men. It should surprise no one, then, that the major issue of this millennium is the status of women coupled with the recognition of their role as essential to the economic and social development, which demands equity and social justice. But this fight for equality is not for a mere abstract ideal of social justice but for the liberation of all humanity, which will take all of us—women and all men. That is why, at the local church level, discriminatory policies must be discarded; they compromise the future of equable communities that truly reflect the kingdom of God and God's intent for humanity. Through an awareness of our common, shared destiny, men and women in the Church must begin to take the initiative to become masters of their future, which means revisiting our practices as informed by the Word.

Based on this premise, this essential question arises: In a world in perpetual turmoil and degradation, how can women transform society and contribute to human liberation? This question, in turn, raises further questions, such as: In the New Testament, and in the history of the Church, where have women laid the foundations of an egalitarian society? As well, how can women offer signs of a hopeful future? This chapter is based on the authority of biblical texts. The method uses historical criticism with an eye toward a feminist theological critique. Church history and feminist research are important, because much of the literature relating to the Church's history about women and their participation in society remains unknown; but there can be no doubt that Jesus Christ saw women as human beings with the same propensities and possibilities as men. This view does not condemn or camouflage sin; on the contrary, it highlights the attributes of women as human. To grasp Jesus's attitude is to turn lives that have been discarded into sources of blessing.

Historical Roles of African Women Leaders

You might be surprised to learn that, historically, women's roles cannot be reduced to stereotypes or typical characterizations as is often the case with African women, what J. Laude portrays as: mother, baby in the back, pounding rice, millet, or cassava.[1] To illustrate, consider Hatshepsut (Egypt, fifteenth century BCE) and the Queen of Sheba (Ethiopia, tenth century BCE), who both imposed themselves on the realm of male power.

Hatshepsut, the heir to Pharaoh Thutmose I, was married to her half brother Thutmose II, so he could become pharaoh. This was done even though she was the child of Thutmose I's primary wife. Thus began the Eighteenth Dynasty. First Wife of the God, Great Royal Bride, Hatshepsut, the Foremost of Noble Ladies, however, was not content to share power according to the tradition. At that time among Egyptians, male and female seem to have been viewed as complementary forces, balanced without antagonism.[2] While some rather misogynistic Egyptologists have been outraged by this, others, less blind, recognize the importance of her exceptional reign.

Benefiting from the conquests of the two previous pharaohs, Hatshepsut inherited an economically and culturally prosperous country. Her influence was not in war, but in planning, construction, commerce, and scientific exploration. Hatshepsut reigned for more than twenty years. She surrounded herself with elite advisors, such as Senenmut, who played a major role.

The Queen of Sheba is another example, and it is not implausible that a great lady would decide to go see King Solomon— builder of the temple, the palace, and other monuments in

---

1   Jean Laude, *Les Arts de l'Afrique Noire* (Paris: Librairie Générale Française, 1966), 298.

2   Jean-Pierre Jacquemin, *Femmes d'Afrique: Grandes Figures Historiques de Femmes, d'Afrique Noire et d'Afrique du Nord, de l'Antiquité à nos Jours* (Bruxelles: Coopération par l'Education et la Culture, 1999), 11.

Jerusalem. The Bible does not tell us her origins,[3] but in Ethiopia she is considered a leading figure and the founder of an African kingdom. Foundational to the story that surrounds her is her characterization as the daughter of the mythical hunter, who delivered his people by ridding the land of the dragon that terrorized them.[4]

According to legend, the Queen of Sheba left her country, accompanied by an impressive entourage, to visit King Solomon. Her visit culminated in a love affair between King Solomon and the Queen. From that relationship, the ancestors of the great Ethiopian dynasties count themselves as heirs, including Haile Selassie and other contemporary Ethiopian leaders. Whether historical or legendary, the Queen of Sheba is still considered influential, and her millennia-old prestige is still reflected in how Ethiopians regard women.

Throughout African history, social and political rights and duties have been determined by gender, which have not necessarily been assigned with male primacy in mind. There have also been times when women's skill and determination have been surprisingly influential. As an example, we can turn to a discussion about Yennega (High Volta, present-day Burkina Faso, twelfth century AD) and Ruwej (Congo, seventeenth century AD).

King Dagomba from the Naba Nedega (an ethnic group from Ghana) had no son, much to his despair. But he had a daughter, Yennega, who was the source of her father's pride. King Dagomba raised Yennega as a boy and introduced her to equestrian arts and the craft of arms. Did this unlikely education stimulate a thirst for independence? Perhaps. One day the princess came into conflict with her father, whose authority hung

---

3   La visite de la Reine de Saba se situe dans le Premier Livre des Rois; 1 R.10, 1-13.

4   Jacquemin, *Femmes d'Afrique*, 13.

over her. Consequently, she chose to flee on horseback and left the kingdom. One night as she wandered, she found herself at the hut of a hunter who welcomed her warmly. From the encounter and later marriage, a son was born, whom she named Ouédraogo, which means "stallion," to honor her horse.[5]

Subsequently she solicited her father's forgiveness and was reconciled with him. Married and the mother of a boy, she restored the patriarchal order that she had inadvertently threatened—everything worked out. Ouédraogo, as an adult, became the leader of conquering riders who, over several centuries, built the four great kingdoms of Fada Ngouma, Yetenga, Tenkodogo, and especially Ouagadougou, which was considered the most prestigious. It is ruled, to this day, by the lineage of kings called Mogho Naba.[6]

Yennega's story, however, left its mark on the institution of the Mossi monarchy. On the death of a Mogho Naba, his oldest daughter, the Napoko, succeeded him in a kind of regency. Symbolically she wore the clothes of the late king, mimicked his public behavior, and withdrew as soon as the royal council appointed the true successor.[7] This ritual probably set the public limits of the female role for traditional power: the role of guardian, guarantor, and mediator.

Yennega, the returning runaway, is still for Burkinabe women the honorable embodiment of organized force, the classic tribute to the mothers of warriors; yet an adventurous and sanctioned

---

5   Lenissongui Coulibaly, *L'Autorité dans l'Afrique Traditionnelle: Etude Comparative des Etats Mossi et Ganda* (Abidjan: Nouvelles Éditions Africaines, 1983), 15.

6   Roger Bila Kabore, *La Princesse Yennega et autres histoire* (Abidjan: Nouvelles Édition Africaines, 1983), 6-8.

7   Kabore, 18.

rebel. Here we see the reversal of this gender role that continues to fascinate the society despite the passage of time.

Then there is the case of Ruwej, to whom was given a lukano bracelet from her father—a sign of authority. As a result, Ruwej met with opposition from her two brothers, who then gave up their claims and left for Angola. The skillful and tenacious young woman refused any local marriage alliance but then shared the lukano with Ilunga Tshibinda, a hunter, who was a member of the dynasty of the well-consolidated neighboring kingdom— the Luba. When she died, having no children of her own, she passed the lukano to her stepson, Yavo Naweji. There were court intrigues, to be sure, but research shows that Yavo was the first emperor (Mwata Yamvo) of the Lunda people (which means friendship) and his stepmother, the first Lukokesh (Queen Mother with real powers). "In memory of Ruwej, the Lukokesh is also named after Swana Mu-Lunda (Mother of Lunda)."[8]

Thanks to the political genius of their founder, the Lunda people made the most of their historical opportunities and constructed a powerful set of alliances, prospering through trade with the Portuguese of Upper Zambese and Angola without being dominated by them. Later, colonization put an end to this remarkable influence, but even today in present-day Katanga, the Mwata Yamvo and Lukokesh still wield undeniable power, and Ruwej's bracelet retains its sovereign strength.

In Tananarive, from the seventeenth century on, a monarchy legitimized by sacred law was established, gradually extending its power to the whole island of Madagascar. In the eighteenth century, Ranavalona I ascended the throne upon the death of her husband, Radama I. "Throughout her reign of thirty-three years,

---

8   Robert Cornevin, *Histoire de l'Afrique: Des Origines à nos Jours* (Paris: Payot, 1956), 288.

she fiercely resisted colonial incursions, fighting with strength and determination for the independence of her people in order to maintain the traditional Malagasy identity."[9] Her death marked the end of this policy and the return of European influence under the reign of her successor.

On the day of her coronation, November 22, 1883, the last sovereign of Madagascar, Ranavalona III, was twenty-two years old. She went to the city of the founding princes to acquire the power of the ancestors. From the top of the sacred stone erected on top of the hill overlooking the city, and in a strangely high-pitched voice, she addressed the silent crowd that surrounded her:

> Here is what I have to say to you, O my people! God gave me this land, God gave me this Kingdom and I thank you for it. The Great Andrianampoinimérina and Radama I, Ranavalona I, Rasoherina, Ranavalona II, have bequeathed me this kingdom as a legacy. Therefore, if anyone wants to take a piece of this land, even a hair, I will put myself forward as if I were a man to defend our common homeland![10]

Unfortunately, she could not keep this promise, because in 1890 when the French took Madagascar, the queen was taken hostage and deported to Algiers, where she was held in captivity until her death in 1917. Thus the colonial invader ended the reign of Ranavalona III.

In Niger, Sarraounia was the daughter of Serkin, the king of the Aznas who led the fight against the slave-trading Tuaregs and the mighty marabouts of Sokoto. Her mother died giving

---

9   Jacquemin, *Femmes d'Afrique*, 38.

10   E. Gerbinis, "L'Intronisation de Ranavalona III," in *Revue de Madagascar*, 1955, no. 24, 39-41.

birth to her. So, from an early age, Sarranouia learned to live as a lone female among men, who nevertheless introduced her to the use of weapons of war and hunting. There she discovered "among the spirits of the Shadow, all the secrets of good and evil, the plants that kill and those that rise, the elixirs of strength and intelligence."[11] At the age of twenty her father died, and she ascended the throne to continue the fight against the "blue men" of the North and the Muslims of the South. The queen urged the fearsome Azna warriors into battle and soon became legendary throughout the Haoussa country and beyond.

A French colonial mission led by Captain Voulet and Lieutenant Chanoine left Ségou for Lake Chad in 1899. There they forcibly enslaved hundreds of men, women, and children to be sold in the markets in Sudan (present-day Mali). Their soldiers razed and plundered towns and villages, massacring the population as they went, ruthlessly sowing terror in their path. Sarraounia fought back by organizing and seeking to rally the neighboring kingdoms. However, they resisted, so she put another strategy in place. After evacuating men, women, and children from the bush, she chose the best warriors, ordered them to smear themselves with a "magical" ointment that would stop bullets, and then waited for the enemy. The result was spectacular. Both Chanoine and Voulet were shot. The soldiers retreated in disbelief and disarray, now living their worst nightmare. Afterward, the capital of the Azna kingdom was rebuilt; but then new invaders emerged, seizing the rulers and raising their flag in the kingdom. As for the queen, she locked herself in her palace only to disappear in the form of a yellow-eyed panther in the bush forever, securing her legend.

---

11 Abdoulaye Mamany, *Sarraounia* (Paris: L'Harmattan, 1980), 54.

This sketch of the history of powerful women in Africa, which emerges from the work of archaeologists and historians over the last ten or twenty years, says much about African women, and we hope that the research continues with many more exciting finds. We now turn to discuss African women in the modern era.

The Contemporary Situation of African Women

The historic presence of women in the structures of traditional African society bears no further explanation. But today, African traditions are under severe strain from social, economic, political, and legal changes. The result is that "a dialectic between tradition and modernity in the form of a tension between what has always been done and the demands of urban life, the lifestyle dictated by state bureaucracy, the market economy or the principles of mass hygiene. There is therefore a tension between tradition and the new demands related to social mobility and the progress of urban civilization, the mixing of populations, education and the media."[12]

Our society is made of a mixture of tradition and modernity, so the question is whether the traditional role of women will continue to grow with the process of modernization of Africa, or whether it is possible to say with T. N'Dri "that after participating in the struggles against colonial powers, women were no longer recognized political actors and therefore could no longer afford to operate in a visible and rewarding way."[13]

---

12 A. M. Yimga, "Conceptions Traditionnelles du Mariage au Cameroun," in *Les Relations Nouvelles entre Hommes et Femmes: Préalable au développe de l'Afrique* (Yaoundé: CLE, 2010), 20.

13 N'Dri Thérèse Assie-Lumumba, *Les Africaines dans la politique: femmes baoulé de Côte d'Ivoire* (Paris: L'Harmattan, 1996), 169.

Political independence is a reasonable historical benchmark to describe the evolution of women's movements in contemporary Africa. Fatou Sow, a student at the University of Dakar in the early years of independence, entered the CNRS (National Center for Scientific Research) and pursued a career as a researcher in sociology, first writing a thesis on Senegalese elites and later receiving authorization to conduct further research. Gradually, her scientific exchanges with colleagues from other countries led her to take an interest in sociological studies of women in African countries, and she became a firm feminist activist.

In addition to Sow's research and teaching activities at the Cheikh Anta Diop University in Dakar, in 1994 she contributed to the creation of an annual Gender Institute at the Council for the Development of Social Sciences in Africa (Codesria) in order to train African researchers on gender issues. She also directed, with Ayesha M. Imam and Amina Mama, the book *Engendering African Social Sciences* (Codesria, 1997), translated and published under the title *Sex, Gender and Society, Empowering the African Social Sciences* (Karthala, 2004). Since 1998, she has pursued a career as a teacher in Dakar and as a researcher at the CNRS, at the University of Paris Diderot, in the study "Society in Space and Time Development" (Sedet), managed by Catherine Coquery-Vidrovitch.

In 1999 Sow organized, again in Dakar, the second symposium of French-language feminist research, whose proceedings were published under the title *The French Feminist Research: Language, Identities and Issues* (Karthala, 2009). The partnerships she developed with American and African universities in the early 1990s allowed her to forge effective links between African feminists in both linguistic areas, French and English. She also had responsibilities in several feminist networks, including as the Francophone Africa coordinator for "Develop-ment Alternatives for Women in a New Era" (DAWN), a power-ful network of southern feminists whose research has been used to lobby international institutions. A member and president of the Reproductive Health Research Network in French-speaking Africa (1994-1996), Sow collaborated with Codou Bop to write *Our Body, Our Health: Women's Health and Sexuality in Sub-Saharan Africa* (Harmattan, 2004). Since 2008 she has been the coordinator of another research and advocacy network, Women Living under Muslim Laws, based in Asia, Africa, and the Middle East.

However, in my opinion, Awa Keita (1975-) is, above all, the symbol of the anti-colonial struggle in French Sudan, like many of the great ancestors we like to celebrate. Awa Keita and even Alin Sito-Diatta of Senegal are figures of resistance to the colonial order rather than symbols of feminism. Above all, they demon-strate the ability of women to resist the colonial order with their political commitment. They are heroes.

New Testament Women as Paradigms

What is the contribution of New Testament women to the con-struction of this new society? By learning about these women, what models can they help create for African women so that women and men in this society are new beings; that they respond to a vision of new equity, peace, and justice in the community?

The Strategy of the Canaanite Woman (Matthew 15:21-28)

This passage in the first Gospel largely echoes the integration of non-Jews into God's plan of salvation. This openness is possible thanks to a woman who, in her suffering (the demonic possession of her daughter), did not let Jesus rest in his retreat. Her cries, entreaties, and humility have made her a figure eager to free herself from all traces of prejudice and complexity in order to get what she needs. What strategies must she use to achieve the desired results?

What matters is the incomprehensible audacity of this unholy gesture in which this woman defies morality and taboos and even makes fun of making unclean this man whom she touches. Consequently, we should be attentive to her bold gesture to determine her means of struggle. The crowd is present and encloses Jesus and his disciples. Fearful and distraught, the woman approaches. We know that it was not customary in that culture for any woman, let alone a Gentile woman, to rub shoulders with a rabbi. It was also the custom that only men taught, and teaching given by men was reserved for men.

All of a sudden this woman inserts herself into Jesus's company and entreats him to heal her daughter. At first Jesus simply ignores her; then his disciples insist that Jesus send her away, giving the message that she is not worth his time and trouble. After all, she is unclean, and any association with her will make Jesus (and by extension, his disciples) unclean as well.[14] However, propelled into dialogue with Jesus because of the needs of her daughter, the woman cannot be deterred, even when Jesus compares her to a χυνάριον, a dog, who, even so, can have a place in the house and crumbs from the table.[15]

When the woman replies that even dogs are given crumbs from the table, she is saying that she does not mean to take

---

14 Andre Wenin and Camille Focant, *Vives: Femmes de la Bible* (Bruxelles: Lessius, 2007), 110.

15 Wenin and Focant, 111.

anything away from those who sit at the table but only glean the extras, the crumbs—what others would discard. In her view, there is more than enough for all.[16] Through this clever turn of the conversation, Jesus catches a glimpse of her faith. Yes, for her, even Jesus's smallest actions are more than enough to fill her need. Just as John 4 tells us that Jesus offers water that will permanently quench our thirst, here we see that even the smallest morsel of bread will satisfy our deepest need.

The Strategy of the Woman with the Hemorrhage (Luke 8:43-48)

Luke tells the story of an encounter by Jesus with another woman who was considered unclean. But this woman bore a curse of an unrelenting issue of blood. When she interrupts Jesus, who is busy meeting the need of an important government official, she is also daring to not only break custom but break a taboo.[17] She does not ask permission to touch Jesus; she simply gets as close as she can and reaches for what she can get—the hem of his garment.

Luke tells us that her disease has been eating away at her for twelve years, marginalizing her and making her culturally unclean. By her incessant flow, she is wounded in her very femininity; she is excluded from worship and all social life, as her life gradually drains out of her. For others to see her as only impure and surely guilty of some grievous sin to be punished in this way, can only be shameful. Her disease has rendered her useless. Her body gives and gives, to excess, without being able to accept healing in

---

16 Wenin and Focant, 111.

17 Alphonse Maillot, *Marie, Ma Sœur: Etude sur la Femme dans le Nouveau Testament* (Paris: Letouzey et Ané, 1990), 41.

return.[18] The fact that she spends from her own livelihood proves that her husband has sent her away with her dowry to fend for herself. She is alone in her suffering and marginalization.

A broken and contaminating object, she approaches, touching Jesus who immediately feels the power go out of him. Just as he brings the official's daughter back to life in the next few verses, here Jesus restores the life of this woman. Her gesture contrasts with the attitude of the crowd and the disciples who press, encircle, and suffocate. The woman's gesture has a special value, for she alone discerns the dynamic power that dwells within Jesus—the live-giving force of salvation. Despite culturally imposed taboos, she knows that he transcends the law and that in him and him alone is life; with him all things become possible. Through touch this brave anonymous woman experiences a personal encounter with Jesus.

Despite the death that swirls around her (Lev 19:26; Deut 12:16), this woman does not reach out blindly to just any source of healing; she comes to touch the One Torrent of Life—Jesus,[19] who in turn is obliged to show fully what he has come to do and bring. It is therefore in peace that she is sent back to this new world that begins for her. With her and through her, menstrual impurity is no longer an obstacle and no longer an excuse for rejection, disgust, contempt, and prohibition.

The Poor Widow as a Model for African Women

Deprived and impoverished, like her fellows, another New Testament woman stands out. Marginalized by scribes who knew how

---

18 Eugen Drewermann, *La Parole et l'angoisse: Commentaire de l'évangile de Marc* (Paris: Desclée de Brouwer, 1995), 113.

19 Maillot, *Marie, Ma Soeur*, 45.

to take advantage of the helpless people, the widow of whom Mark speaks (Mark 12:41-44) gives all of what little she has. She offers God her whole life, thus aligning herself with the evangelistic message. Can this widow serve as a model for African women despite their continual exploitation?

The answer is yes, as evidenced by their many responsibilities, because we must not forget that women play an increasingly remarkable role in our modern society. Because of the increasing importance of the political sphere, women also have a great influence on the public affairs of African countries. Despite food insecurity, rural women have proved that they are still able to give, and regarding this the example of Côte d'Ivoire is revealing.[20]

Indeed, the food crisis has made it possible to appreciate the know-how of women who, despite sociocultural obstacles and despite a difficult political and economic environment, have filled the vacuum created by male unemployment. Women are creating informal new income-generating activities on all fronts to help provide for the survival of their families, thus becoming the pillars of communities.

Under the heavy weight of economic crises with wars with their procession of refugees and violence that continues to shake Africa, the family model built on the primacy of male power is cracking, decaying, and exposing increasingly unbearable contradictions from the point of equity, of justice. This changing socioeconomic situation demands that gender relations must evolve, giving women more freedom. Qualities that can contribute to lasting peace—tenderness, gentleness, love, patience—are often seen as feminine, but they are also considerable assets

---

20 Extraits du plan National d'Action de la Femme, Décembre 2002.

to our society that will allow women to play a leading role in creating a culture of peace, one that promotes human rights, once so revered and now shattered by tribal violence. These qualities promote listening and constructive dialogue with others.

Mary, the Mother of Jesus as a Model for African Women

In a society that is searching for meaning,[21] there is an urgent, pressing need to define new values for life, for human dignity. In John 2 we read the story of the wedding at Cana. Here we see Mary, who is surely dazzled by the actions of her son, Jesus. The text specifies that the disciples waited to believe, while Mary believes even before seeing, before Jesus performs the miracle of turning water into wine. In Mary we see confidence and hope, a commitment to actively engage, and a burning desire to live together. These are characteristics and attitudes that are vital to the success of a peaceful future, peace that can only be achieved through partnership with women.[22] Carrying out an irreversible program for peace and stability in our countries is the major challenge that must be faced, so that constant conflict will cease.[23]

The Strength of African Women

How can we say that we value the traditional role of modern women when we treat them as inferior? Often from daybreak to well beyond dark, a woman will bag the grain, stack the bags in piles, prepare meals, and wash children; yet she is not a prisoner.

---

21 I. Garlander, *Une société en quête de sens* (Paris: Odile Jacob, 1995).
22 E. Mvie Meka, Op. Cit. 31.
23 F. Durieux, *Les Grands faits de l'histoire* (Paris: Clartés, 1987), 31.

She may even have the means to circumvent these duties; still, every day, she goes out to fetch wood and haul water from the well, the river, or even the market.

The market, however, is a privileged meeting place, which transpires on a dependable and, usually, reliable schedule. But getting there sometimes requires women to travel enormous distances, so women go together. The market where women shop or sell their own agricultural produce (onions, tomatoes, peanuts, cassava, etc.) is also the meeting place of a completely different kind. It is not only the place where you find everything you want to buy, but also, and above all, women find the opportunity to start conversations and negotiations concerning joint projects. Finally, she collects information that she will share with those in her village. She can learn about political, religious, economic, and climate news from nearby regions and chiefdoms regarding celebrations, droughts, famine, grasshopper invasions, epidemics or other calamities, good rains, or family get-togethers involving distant friends or relatives (birth, marriage, abduction, flight of women, travel, illness, death).[24]

Women's Power to Name Themselves

In a patriarchal social order, women and their bodies are considered capital. Both men and women give in to this social conditioning, which then becomes social norms and, consequently, characteristic of relationships in a particular society. In this way, women's bodies are exploited and seen as worth the investment, depending on the circumstances. Nevertheless, every woman

---

24 C. et B. Desjeux et D. Bonnet, *Africaines* (Paris: L'Harmattan, 1983), 10.

knows that her body cannot be exploited forever, because, like every living being, her body grows old and eventually dies.

However, a major asset for African women is that they are not only perishable bodies that perpetuate life but also a spirit, a soul, who creates, thinks, imagines, organizes, and has her own values.[25] At a time when the dominant ideology constructs the essential characteristics, defects, and qualities of women and men, sex is a given, even if it is changeable these days. In the life of African women, everything revolves around the forbidden, essential part of body capital: sex, the object of all transactions. Sex is foundational and is the difference between men and women even before society gets involved.

In many customs, when a woman reaches "a certain age" and can no longer give birth, she enters into a special case and can be trusted with prerogatives otherwise reserved for men. In some cases (in the Samo of Upper Volta), infertility is linked to the exercise of political power. As a holder of political power, she is considered a "woman-man."[26] The older a woman gets, the more power she has, as she gradually moves from being a reproductive woman to a woman-man. This woman-man is a counselor, a wise man, and she participates in the council of elders.

Enhancement of the body also involves clothing, hairstyle, and makeup, which are also part of the social construct of sex. How one dresses and wears one's hair are indications of the status of married women and girls. For example, the loincloth doesn't just cover the body; rather this single piece of fabric,

---

25 Tanella Boni, *Que vivent les femmes d'Afrique* (n.p.: Divers, 2008), 39.
26 Evelyne Sullerot, *La femme dans les systèmes de représentation, entretien de F. Heritier*, in Evelyne Sullerot, *Le fait féminin, qu'est-ce qu'une femme* (Paris: Fayard, 1978), 401.

whether short or long, is a language, a means of expression and communication. In addition, the motifs printed on loincloths, even today, are not purely decorative or meant as an aesthetic. They carry meaning. This allows us to say that to understand African women, we must be able to read and decode their loincloths, dresses, and boubous.[27] The design elements on clothing appeal to women, not only because they are beautiful, but because they serve as supports for the expression of their desires, misfortunes, or happiness. Through their dress and other enhancements, women manage sexuality and the roles assigned to them by their society. But every woman needs to be aware of what she may unknowingly communicate, so that she can make better, more prudent decisions. And we must recognize the power of these communications by bringing about conscious awareness, so that silence is broken and, consequently, women can be free to make their own decisions regardless of social constraints.

African women, at times, have shown autonomy in creative initiatives, sovereignty in daily life, and mature judgments that escape men's interference. Women are not victims of cultural assimilation or natural assimilation and must continue to escape such. Women in this context help us all look forward to the dawn of a new day.

A New Day

The vision of a new humanity in Jesus Christ refers to shared responsibility and reciprocity. Reciprocal relationships have an egalitarian basis and advocate for collegial leadership and

---

27 Boni, *Que vivent les femmes d'Afrique*, 27.

power-sharing. On the basis of African values, conviviality, peaceful coexistence, and reciprocity should be promoted in the Church.

A New Humanity and African Women

The Gospels bear witness to the presence of women; Jesus welcomes them and establishes equality between man and woman, in that he disciples both. He gives women, in particular, a new place and a new role. He frees them from the inside. In the name of this kind of liberation, full participation of women will result in the conversion of the Church and the articulation of a new theology that promotes the liberation of all God's people.

Women's Determination to Execute the Vision of New Humanity in Jesus Christ

In the present order of things, does Divine Providence not lead us to a new order of human relationships in which we are always in the presence of a Church? It is not a question of denying some among us but of building with and for each other (Ps 133). Engaging together is linked to God's gift of community, but community marked by certain characteristics as given by God's Word. Without this kind of community, there can be no true loving relationships.[28]

By using new capacities acquired by women through their access to education, political responsibilities, and economic independence, the Church should offer the world tangible proof of women's testimony and service. God made a magnificent gift to humanity through the creation of men and women. We must

---

28 C. Faure, "Le Recrutement au Ministère" in *Flambeau* (Février, 1964), 20.

recognize and give thanks for the meaning and consequences of this duality. The liberation that Christ provided gives us ever new possibilities for increased and healthy self-esteem and fellowship.

The objective is threefold: first, women must carefully distinguish the authentic divine revelation strictly said in relation to all the sociocultural and religious traditions where this revelation has manifested itself. Women also need to study how far the power of the Church extends itself and its possible legitimacy to use the ability to create new traditions, a faculty not yet exercised for various reasons. Second, proclaim the joy and freedom that God has reserved for all—all women and all men—and help everyone discover their true identity in Jesus Christ. Third, live in the Spirit. Refuse to be dry trees, but live fruitfully and faithfully here on earth (John 15).

It is up to us to work toward these possibilities of renewal so that our families, the Church, and everyone else can flourish where God has placed us.

The Realization of the Divine Promises

Christianity plays an important role in raising awareness of the intolerable condition of women in many societies, and it supports movements for the advancement of women as well as for communities that are characterized by equality, reciprocity, and partnership between the genders.

The Effective Involvement of African Women to Invest in Spaces of Complementarity

It is a question of committing to build communities together, while respecting difference and knowing there are limits to human existence (Ps 133). Building this kind of faith community requires deliberate decisions by men and women. While we cannot deny obstacles or difficulties, or even possible failure, we can and must believe that God's love, as manifested in us, has the strength to address these challenges through mutual and profound consent! Commitment is not a question of knowledge or individual voluntarism, but one of faith and trust in the other and oneself and ultimately in God.

In our traditional societies, E. Mvemg introduces us in another dimension of complementarity: the one where man discovers himself as dyad in its double dimension, man-woman. He wrote: "It is in this double dimension that man is fulfilled as a person. There is no opposition, no conflict, no gender equality: there is only complementarity. The man without the woman is nothing: the woman without the man is nothing either. But they are all in their complementarity."[29]

When people accept themselves in this double dimension, they can attain love, creativity, and fertility. He becomes a triad, father-mother-child. She becomes mother-father-child. It is in this triple dimension that humanity is like no other species. Our humanity is portrayed in roots that speak to our relationality.

To be human requires relationships. Alone we are not persons. We only find our true selves when we are in relationship. We cannot be accomplished and balanced persons without others in the context of a social environment. That is why women need to work with other women, with men, in families, and in society—to achieve change. The essential task is no longer to safeguard tradition but to pave the way for innovation, even in the sector where old habits are particularly rooted, as in private life.

---

29 E. Mvemg, *L'art d'Afrique Noire,* 2nd ed. (Yaoundé: Clé, 1974), 13.

New problems due to changes in traditional society will now arise. Once prepared to play their roles in a specific setting and context, many people now find themselves distraught at impending changes. New situations require a sustained and adaptive effort. New situations create new needs and make the education of children difficult. Traditional market economies often want to depend on the goodwill of the husband alone, who sometimes sacrifices the family budget and the interests of his family to his own selfish whims. This influence of men on the economic status of the family and women reinforces the subordination of women. However, women will not remain passive but take all kinds of measures to change their condition. Gradually, a movement of awareness is rising among women who are beginning to take part in social, cultural, and even political activities in countries.

Subordination inflicts many ills on women. But my observation is that many of their causes seem related to the ideology of the hierarchy between the masculine and the feminine. Legal instruments that can bring about change through an awareness of women's rights and a change in mentality are not always taken into account in states. Women are still seen as inferior, malleable beings, and an object of exchange in families.

The question of inferiority in contemporary society makes it difficult to negotiate the transition from traditionalism and modernism, for example, new forms of the guardianship of women. The question arises whether it is possible to highlight the intrinsic value accorded to women in the African tradition and translate it into all the acts of daily life. "It is precisely in the very vision of femininity as a creative energy that the will to eliminate all discrimination against women will be asserted."[30] In doing so, it would be

---

30 Helene Yinda et Ka Mana, *Manifeste de la Femme Africaine: Contre le Système de Violence Envers les Femmes et Pour un Nouveau Chemin*

in line with both traditional and modern societies and could transcend all the stereotypes imposed on them. Social consciousness must be guided in this direction; therefore, we want to study all its contours to offer pathways of liberation to women.

For African women, meeting the challenges remains an important quest; it is a matter of taking possession of land, markets, and kitchens, and tracing the furrows of the future. Consequently, they cannot remain immobile. Women must be on the move, dealing with several things at once. The place for African women is not devoid of other people but where relationships of all kinds are forged, where life is difficult and disturbing, where death that runs the streets is not only literal but figurative. Every woman is unique, and she will fill her places as she sees fit.

Conclusion

In different civilizations women can be considered emancipated in domestic life. These societies were once marked by social collectivism, a material and moral solidarity. Even today, this conception of women and society extends into traditional African life. Yet many see women in their daily life as being treated as "less than"—less than men. They say this is done to ensure her progeny, perhaps to pay a debt to family members by extending their lineage. In this way, men assure their superiority over women, hence reinforcing their relationships as hierarchical, with women cast as subordinate and inferior. But today, as one views traditional African life, it goes without saying that most of these preconceived ideas and social constructs have become inadequate.

---

d'Humanité (Bafoussam: CIPCRE, 2005), 28.

In the realities of daily life, which should not be overestimated, we see human flourishing, especially of women. Their secret aspirations are neither stifled nor repressed. Society gives an acceptable degree of individual freedom, and the relationship between the sexes is orderly. And as the degree of a civilization is measured by the relationship between men and women, traditional society can be seen as one that has the potential to liberate women. Women in this context have value.

Now that the essence of traditional society is uncovered, one can better appreciate the conception of women in modern society. The observation of the facts reveals the breakdown of the harmony between men and women. Modern design breaks the relative independence of women. It has closed the floodgates of the feminine consciousness, while opening and exalting men to their highest degree. Women lose the substance of their traditional value in modernism. The problem of inferiority arises acutely. Women engage in the struggle to find their lost value, and they engage in many struggles for their dignity but to no avail because the drama comes from the previously acquired habits; you don't clean up your consciousness with a sponge.

The challenges remain numerous and the fight continues. What can I do? Can the reference to New Testament women breathe new life and set straight the relationship between men and women?

THREE

Who Is "She" in Ecclesiastes 7:26?

An Alternative Reading against Cultural Biases

ELAINE WEI-FUN GOH, THD

F emme fatale" is a phrase that originated in French and is widely used to describe a compellingly attractive woman who leads men into disastrous outcomes.[1] A historical example is Cleopatra III as well as biblical figures such as Delilah. A legendary example from Chinese primeval history and literature is Daji.[2] Ever after, *femme fatale* or "snake-scorpion beauty" (*shexie meiren*) in Mandarin, has become an archetype of any charming

---

1   This chapter is an adaptation and a shorter version from an article by the same author, used with permission of the publisher, "She Is More Bitter Than Death: Reading Ecclesiastes 7:23–8:1 as an Asian Chinese," in Jione Havea and Peter H. W. Lau, eds., *Reading Ecclesiastes in Asia and Pasifika* (Atlanta: SBL Press, 2020).

2   Daji is featured in the Chinese novel *Fengshen Yanyi*, which is a collection of many legendary characters and stories from ancient China. Daji, a beautiful but wicked woman, was the favourite concubine of King Zhou of the Shang Dynasty in ancient China. She is notoriously

yet dangerous woman in the common narratives and mindset of Asian Chinese.[3]

The idea of a "snake-scorpion beauty" naturally comes to mind when an Asian Chinese reads Ecclesiastes 7:26, "I found the woman more bitter than death."[4] Who is *the woman* in Ecclesiastes 7:26? Is she an actual woman whom Qoheleth intended to identify? This chapter argues for a metaphorical interpretation in the light of Proverbs 1–9. It seeks to differ that biblical readers influenced by Chinese culture connect Ecclesiastes 7:26 to a real "snake-scorpion beauty" too presumably, as this may be colored by Chinese cultural biases.

Chinese Cultural Biases

Chinese culture has long been observed to have generated ideas and conceptions of femininity in a negative light. The Chinese people believe that males are dominant, powerful, and associated with *yang* (meaning, "masculinity"). Women, on the other hand, are the opposite—submissive, weak, and best described as *yin* (meaning, "femininity"). Against this worldview, oppressive social expectations were permitted at the expense of females; for instance, the acceptance of polygamy in Chinese

---

cruel and is related to a malevolent fox spirit with nine tails by later generations.

3   The author is from Chinese ethnicity yet was born and raised in Malaysia. Therefore, the term "Chinese" in this chapter is rendered culturally, rather than nationally. In this chapter, "Chinese" usually refers to a social identity with related cultural heritage but never refers to China, the country.

4   English translations in this paper are mine, unless otherwise stated.

history. A husband with many wives was considered acceptable, and is still common.

Female historian and scholar Ban Zhao (45-120 CE) helped shape four main virtues of women as social norms. In her book *Nüjie* (*Admonitions for Women*), she advocated for women's virtue (*fude*), women's speech (*fuyan*), women's appearance (*furong*), and women's work (*fugong*).[5] She believed that women should be conservative, humble, and quiet. Women should also express ritual or filial propriety as their virtue.[6] Similarly, a woman's speech should not be forceful or swaying but soft and prudent; she should also pay close attention to her appearance and act sensibly in public.[7] Against this basic idea, any woman who is the direct opposite of the above is deemed to be wicked and dreadful. Therefore, Ecclesiastes 7:26, "I found the woman more bitter than death," creates an image that "the woman" embraces snakes and scorpions and has a fox's spirit. Chinese thinking is fundamentally gendered and often biased.

Ecclesiastes 7:23-8:1 on Seeking Wisdom

The theme that runs through Ecclesiastes 7:23-8:1 is seeking wisdom. There is a chiastic structure in this passage. It begins with testing wisdom (7:23-25) and ends with having wisdom (8:1). Sandwiched in between the frame is 7:26-29, which elaborates on avoiding folly.

---

5   Lijuan Shen and Paul D'Ambrosio, "Gender in Chinese Philosophy," in *Internet Encyclopedia of Philosophy*, internet resources, accessed 3/11/2019, https://iep.utm.edu/gender-c/.

6   Shen and D'Ambrosio.

7   Shen and D'Ambrosio.

A   7:23-25   Testing wisdom

B   7:26-29   Avoiding folly

A'   8:1   Having wisdom

In this passage the verb "find," *mäcä´*, appears eight times (verses 24, 26, 27 [twice], 28 [three times], and 29), making nine occurrences total in the chapter, when including Ecclesiastes 7:14. It is rather clear that Qoheleth is trying to find out something. The verb *mäcä´* is significant, as it is the very word used in the wisdom circle to promote the idea of seeking wisdom (e.g., Prov 2:4-5; 3:13; 8:8, 18, 35; 19:8). In the language of personification, pursuing wisdom is likened to pursuing a woman of noble character (Prov 18:22; 31:10)—she is more prized than precious stones! A decent woman is an ideal wife.

Testing Wisdom (7:23-25)

Qoheleth has tested (*näsâ*) his life with pleasure (2:1), and here in 7:23 he says he has tested (*näsâ*) "all" with wisdom. Even though Qoheleth is a sage, wisdom becomes a stranger to him at times, just as 7:23 suggests. Qoheleth challenges anyone who can find out the things that are far off and very deep (v. 24). Qoheleth has nevertheless attempted to find them out; therefore in verse 25 he compounds his search with recurring infinitives like *knowing* (twice), *searching*, and *seeking*.

The next four nouns in 7:25 are the opposites of wisdom: wickedness (*reša´*), folly (*Kesel*), foolishness (*hassiklût*), and madness (*hôlëlôt*); among which, only "foolishness" (*hassiklût*) has a definite article. This definite article is significant, as it will affect how one understands "the woman" (*hä´iššâ*) in verse 25, which also comes with a definite article. Qoheleth warns of wisdom's opposites right here, and one who seeks wisdom must know the differences between wisdom and folly. In the following verses, Qoheleth illustrates the real struggles with which one has to wrestle in order to stay away from folly.

Avoiding Folly (7:26-29)

Qoheleth asserts that one would encounter "the woman" and that "she is more bitter than death" (7:26). Why would Qoheleth abruptly bring up a subject of woman, especially one that is preceded by the definite article (*hä´iššâ*)? There is no earlier mention of woman in the book, although it is twice mentioned after (7:28 and 9:9). Qoheleth seems to expect the readers know who "the woman" is. Needless to say, Qoheleth and his readers of the wisdom tradition were familiar with wisdom etymology.

The association of wisdom with a female embodiment is common in the book of Proverbs. The sages employ the metaphor of a good woman to illustrate wisdom, as the word "wisdom" is a feminine noun (e.g., Prov 1:20-33; 3:13-18; 4:6-9). On the other hand, the sages also use the metaphor of a wicked woman to illustrate folly (e.g., 5:1-6; 7:6-27; 9:13-18). And here, Qoheleth warns about the reality of folly. This word *hä´iššâ* (the woman) connects to *hassiklût* (foolishness) in 7:25, where it is the only noun with a definite article. Therefore, "the woman" in verse 26 is not just any woman or a specific woman in reality. "The woman" who is more bitter than death is wisdom's opposite. "She" is Lady Folly.

Besides being described as more bitter than death, Lady Folly is further said to be a trap (*hî´ mücôdîm*); her heart is snares and nets, and her hands are fetters (7:26). The heart in the human body represents one's motive, which is hidden, and the hand denotes one's action, which is visible. Therefore, the passage describes Lady Folly as dangerous both inside and out.

One who has wisdom is one who pleases God and is also one who escapes from Lady Folly. Conversely, the one who does not possess wisdom (the sinner!) is entrapped in her nets and fetters.

Nevertheless, it is noteworthy that the proposition of Michael V. Fox on this passage is indicative for an alternate reading.[8] Fox has maintained that the woman referenced in this passage is an actual woman and that the passage is inevitably misogynistic.[9] In spite of this, Qoheleth may not intend his remarks here to be taken with too much gravity. Fox is certain that Qoheleth does not defend the honor of women, yet Qoheleth does not think too highly of men either. Further, Qoheleth's comments on woman-kind in 7:26 resemble what is advocated in the book of Proverbs about the adulterous strange woman (e.g., Prov 22:14).[10] Fox's suggestion, in my opinion, points to one who prefers to take "the woman" literally (not metaphorically) to read in line with Proverbs on one hand and to read in the light of how men and humanity are described in Ecclesiastes on the other. Fox himself concludes (at the end this passage) that Qoheleth is "speaking of a flaw common to humanity generally."[11]

At least three difficulties exist in Ecclesiastes 7:26-29. First, the notion "I found (*mäcä'tî*) yet I have not found (*lö' mäcä'tî*)" is observed in verse 27 and in the first half of verse 28. It is repeated in the second half of verse 28, which reads: "One man among a thousand I found, but a woman among all these I have not found" (NRSV). The connection of 7:28b with 7:28a is not obvious. It is an abrupt comparison between a man and a woman, as one would

---

8   Michael V. Fox, *A Time to Tear Down and a Time to Build Up: A Rereading of Ecclesiastes* (Grand Rapids, MI: Eerdmans, 1999), 269.

9   Fox, 267.

10 Fox, 269.

11 Fox, 272.

expect a comparison between wisdom and folly instead—"One foolish person among a thousand I found, but a wise among all these I have not found." To do away with its ambiguity, I agree with Leong Seow that this verse can be better posited as Qoheleth actually seeks Lady Wisdom, believing that she can deliver him from the traps and snares of Lady Folly, only to realize that he has not found Lady Wisdom.[12] Her elusive presence has troubled Qoheleth.

Second, there is a perplexing grammatical issue of gender in 7:27. The verb "says" (*'āmrâ*) is in feminine form, as if for Qoheleth the subject is a female. The verb nevertheless appears in masculine form in 1:2 and 12:8 (*'āmar*). All three verses mentioned here have a similarity; nonetheless, they represent the voice of the narrator in the book.

Third, a greater difficulty lies in the word *'ādām* (usually translated as "man") in 7:28b, "One man among a thousand I found, but a woman among all these I have not found." If a man (male) is meant in the word *'ādām* in 7:28b, Qoheleth could have used *'iš* instead. Yet Qoheleth's usage of *'ādām* refers to humanity throughout the whole book, not just male. Therefore, since *'ādām* is used here, the comparison in this verse should be between a human and a woman, rather than between a man and woman. Further, when *'ādām* recurs in the next verse (v. 29), it is clear that "humanity" is meant in "God made *humanity* upright, yet they have sought for many schemes." Although the comparison between humanity and a woman in 7:28b is bizarre, it becomes clearer when the "woman" here is understood as personified wisdom. I suggest, therefore, that Qoheleth is actually saying, "One *human* among a thousand I found, but *wisdom* among all these (seeking), I have not found."

---

12 Choon-Leong Seow, *Ecclesiastes* (New York: Doubleday, 1997), 68-69.

This proposal is significant for one to understand 7:27-29. At base, it solves the difficulties that come along with the use of *'ādām*. At best, it corrects a notorious misinterpretation of this text—that Qoheleth the male chauvinistic sage teaches to devalue females. We have encountered people who have used this passage as a support for a gender-biased standpoint; and therefore promote an idea that an upright woman is impossible to find, because God has solely made men upright! The woman who is mentioned in verse 26 and the imageries of a trap, nets, and fetters related to her could further be taken to enhance such a view. In short, 7:28b poses interpretive difficulties in close reading. Taken at face value, it will create gender-biased misunderstanding.[13]

Consequently, Qoheleth has finally found (*mācā´*) a conclusion in 7:29 that "God made *humanity* upright, yet they have sought for many schemes." The ninth occurrence of the verb *mācā´* recollects what Qoheleth has been seeking—wisdom to understand certain truth in life. Qoheleth realizes two things. First, God has made humanity upright; and this will rhetorically echo verse 13, "See the work of God, who is able to straighten what he has made crooked?" Second, humanity has made things crooked by many "schemes" (*hiššübönôt*). Qoheleth points out the problem with humanity in verse 29, that is, their tendency to oppose God's will. In Bartholomew's word, "it is not the world that is crooked but humans," and human's quest for autonomy

---

13 Seow, *Ecclesiastes,* 265. Seow suggests, to solve the difficulty, there is a possibility that 7:28b represents an insertion by the narrator, just as the third person's "Qohelet says" in verse 27. The insertion may be a personal opinion or the narrator's interpretation of 7:28a. As such, verse 29 continues the sequence of thought from 7:28a.

opposes their dependence on God.[14] Seeking truth and meaning in life away from God is foolish. This may have caused Qoheleth to utter a sense of vanity in life many times in Ecclesiastes.

In the pursuit of wisdom all humanity including Qoheleth himself has fallen into circumstances of foolishness instead. Wisdom is elusive indeed, just as Qoheleth has been wrestling to comprehend it fully.

Having Wisdom (8:1)

The theme of seeking wisdom runs through till 8:1, where Qoheleth presents two rhetorical questions to end this passage. It is remarkable that Qoheleth did not begin by asking, "Who is the wise?" Since wisdom is difficult to hold on to (7:29), the question is, "Who is *like* the wise?" And further, "Who knows the solution of a matter?" These questions are rhetorical as Qoheleth expects "no one" as the answer. The flow of thought from 7:26-29 is, therefore, consistent.

Wisdom's benefits come next: it makes one's face shine, and it changes the hardness of one's countenance. In Ecclesiastes 8:1 a shining face conveys a kind of divine blessedness (cf. Numbers 6:25). Wisdom, after all, can make a difference to a person's life. It transforms a person's attitude and makes a person more amiable—if only one can have it!

Understanding Biblical Feminine Metaphor

Wisdom becomes "alive" in the teaching of the sages. She— Lady Wisdom—will lead the seeking ones to the path of blessings

---

14 Craig G. Bartholomew, *Ecclesiastes*, Baker Commentary on the Old Testament, Wisdom and Psalms, ed. Tremper Longman III (Grand Rapids, MI: Baker Academic, 2009), 175.

and longevity. Conversely, folly is characterized as a seductive woman. She—Lady Folly—is ready to take on young men to the path of self-destruction. Obviously, a noble woman is a metaphor for wisdom; and a seductress, a metaphor for foolishness. These are biblical representations and are unique in wisdom tradition. Doubtless, the metaphors have derived from ancient Israelites' households and social interaction. Nevertheless, direct adaptation and application by Chinese interpreters may miss the point. If a biblical reader from Chinese culture associates Lady Folly with any historical or cultural character, the interpretation can be flawed, as it may be informed—or misinformed—through cultural biases.

When reading wisdom texts one needs to discern that the wisdom tradition disseminates wisdom through the personified Lady Wisdom. Wisdom's embodiment is in feminine form as the gender of the noun suggests. She is an ideal wife to have, and her value is far more precious than jewels. Therefore, Lady Wisdom is worth pursuing wholeheartedly. For dialectic purpose, the sages also create a metaphor of wisdom's opposite, Lady Folly. She conversely is an embodiment of an immoral and seductive woman. The sages warn against her deception and the danger that will lead to grievous harm. The theological message is clear: one who chooses Lady Wisdom will get life, and one who follows Lady Folly will face death.

In short, wisdom and folly become alive in Wisdom Literature. If one were to read Ecclesiastes 7:23–8:1 in the light of personified wisdom and folly, one would not miss the intended metaphorical meaning of "the woman" in 7:26, whom Qoheleth avers that "she is more bitter than death." This comes from a frustration after Qoheleth has launched a desperate grasp for wisdom, yet to no avail. In Craig Bartholomew's word, "Clearly these imageries are intended to evoke the inaccessibility of wisdom."[15] As Peter Enns also suggests, the concluding section of this passage indicates Qoheleth's appeal to the sages who have written Proverbs 1-9, "Show me, because I have not found her."[16]

In my opinion, Ecclesiastes 7:23-8:1 can be juxtaposed to Proverbs 31:10-31. As the capable woman in Proverbs 31:10-31 is hard to find, wisdom is likewise beyond grasp in Ecclesiastes 7:23-8:1. While Lady Wisdom is more precious than jewels in Proverbs, Lady Folly is more bitter than death in Ecclesiastes. The connection between this woman in Ecclesiastes 7:26-29 and the woman in Proverbs 31 has long been suggested.[17] One can put it more ironically that Qoheleth is unable to find wisdom despite all his seeking, and Qoheleth's quest of Lady Wisdom has poignantly led him into the arms of Lady Folly.[18]

Conclusion

The governing idea of Ecclesiastes 7:23-8:1 is Qoheleth's focus on seeking wisdom. Therefore, logically, the woman described as "more bitter than death" is wisdom's opposite. She is Lady Folly, the personified folly. This understanding is consistent in the metaphorical portrayal of folly in the book of Proverbs. Reading the passage as a whole, Qoheleth's failure in his quest for wisdom lies in the foolishness of human schemes to go against God's intention.

---

15 Bartholomew, 265-66.

16 Peter Enns, *Ecclesiastes*, The Two Horizons Old Testament Commentary (Grand Rapids, MI: Eerdmans Publishing, 2011), 88-89.

17 See Al Wolters, *The Song of the Valiant Woman: Studies in the Interpretation of Proverbs 31:10-31* (Carlisle, UK: Paternoster, 2001), 93.

18 See, for example, Bartholomew, *Ecclesiastes*, 268.

This chapter suggests that one must guard one's cultural biases when reading biblical wisdom text and has offered an alternative reading, especially to biblical interpreters of Chinese origin particularly in Asia. Informed by culturally generated understanding, the woman who is "more bitter than death" in Ecclesiastes 7:26 could be hastily read as an actual person that Qoheleth has encountered in his life of vapor; for instance, the "snake-scorpion beauty" to be read as Qoheleth's wife. As a matter of fact, the biblical text in general and Wisdom Literature in particular, has a wealth of feminine imageries and metaphors that speak otherwise.

FOUR

The Challenges of Women in Ministry

Women's Participation in Pastoral Leadership at the United Methodist Church in Mozambique

HELENA ANGELICA GUSTAVO GUIDIONE, BD

Mozambican society is undergoing significant economic, social, and demographic transformations. Therefore, there is a growing participation of women in the labor market and, in particular, The United Methodist Church. There are now a considerable number of women pastors in pastoral ministry, some holding prominent positions in Church leadership in various sectors. Despite our gains, we still live in a society that is dominated by patrilineal culture, with some similar patriarchal characteristics described in the Old Testament. This chapter is a critical study of attitudes toward women in southern Mozambique, who are seen and treated as inferior. In this part of the world women are regarded as only being capable of caring for the house, the children, and the husband. They are without rights to make decisions in the family or in the sectors in which they work, even when they work without remuneration. At the same time, however, women in ministry have a leadership role. So the question becomes, how is this possible when, by definition, at least culturally, women are not leaders and are deemed incapable of leadership?

Given the importance and the high regard with which people of southern Mozambique hold the Bible, this chapter will examine some women in the Old and New Testaments as possible models for our African patriarchal context. Even in the patriarchal contexts of the Old and New Testaments, women fulfilled leadership roles and were viewed as capable beyond the familial sphere. Perhaps a critical look at the Bible can offer new possibilities for African women today.

Introduction

Some women in pastoral leadership roles receive little social acceptance. How can this be, given the importance of the Church? And how can the Church help change society and improve the status and role of women's leadership? To address these questions I will use historical-critical methods to examine some women in the Bible. Then I will compare their stories with modern-day women in southern Mozambique. While the biblical and African contexts are different, to be sure, there is also a lot that is the same. The chauvinist mentalities that we see demonstrated in the Bible are still very much alive, making it difficult for today's woman in ministry to lead and be the leader that God has called her to be.

Women in the Old Testament

The Bible begins with God's speaking creation into being. As part of that work, God creates men and women in God's image.

Both are created, and one is not prioritized above the other. Genesis 1:26-27 reads: And God said,

> Let us make humankind in our image, according to our likeness; and let them have dominion over the fish of the sea, and over the birds of the air, and over the cattle, and over all the wild animals of the earth, and over every creeping thing that creeps upon the earth. So God created humankind in his image, / in the image of God he created them; / male and female he created them.

Although this Bible passage was written at a time when women were considered inferior, these verses do not tout the superiority of men. According to the writer this passage expresses quite the opposite. The entry of sin in the world and not God's intention causes the misalignment and rift in the relationship between men and women.

Even though women are praised in Proverbs, and even Song of Songs, there can be no doubt that women typically were not regarded as full persons with full legal standing. And while it is possible that at times Israelite/Jewish women may have had more legal protections than women of other cultures, the fact remains that Israelite women were seen as "less than." In fact men thanked God daily that they were not born women, Gentiles, or slaves.

However, we also read in Exodus that Miriam was a religious leader, a prophetess, of the people who celebrated their liberation from the Egyptian taskmasters in dance and song. Deborah was a judge (Judg 4) who ruled Israel. Huldah, the wife of Shallum (2 Chron 34:22) was a prophetess. Even Abigail, on behalf of the household, made the decision to disavow her husband Nabal and follow, and later marry, David (1 Sam 25). These women were leaders in their own right and led their people in the paths of the Lord.

The Place of Women in the New Testament

We also read about the prophetess Anna (Luke 2:36) who recognized Jesus for who he was, thus playing her part in the history of salvation.

In the New Testament it is clear that Jesus takes a view of women that differs from his context. For him, men and women are valued equally. We can see this because Jesus invited both men and women to listen to his teaching; we find Jesus inviting women to follow him on his mission, where he preached and proclaimed the word of God (Mark 15:40-41; Luke 8:1-3). By even offering an invitation to follow him, something that women traditionally did not do, he breaks with the usual patriarchal way of life. The presence of Jesus awakes women's potential. We can clearly see this in his encounter with the woman at the well (John 4). Here he offers the woman living water, which she accepts. Then, in an act of evangelism, she returns to her village and brings many people back with her to see and hear Jesus. Throughout the New Testament, as in this case, women are not only hearers of the Word, but also messengers of the Word, demonstrating courage and strength. And we can remember that while the male disciples hid in fear after the crucifixion, it was women who first went to the tomb; women who first witnessed the risen Christ; women who were given the authority to first share the good news and inform the male disciples (Matt 28). In a society that had men's interests first and foremost in mind, Jesus instituted change by offering respect for women and giving them jobs to do in his name.

Women's participation as followers of Jesus demonstrates his rejection of discriminatory laws and customs that belittled women. Jesus risked his prestige and gave his life for all—men and women equally—thus forming a new community where men and women can be equally involved, be equally valued, and each lead.

Women in The United Methodist Church Leadership

Women's participation in The United Methodist Church leadership has brought profound change in Mozambican society. Through the teachings and doctrine of the Church, women are more aware of their value and possibilities, including leadership in pastoral ministry, without losing their own place in the society. Pastoral ministry does not diminish a woman's responsibility; she is still committed to taking care of the home, children, and her husband. But leadership in the Church gives her greater responsibility, even if, due to gender inequality, her leadership role is unrecognized or is undervalued.

Yet inequality persists. We see this in the writings of Leonardo Pinheiro, who insists that "the man is the head of the household and responsible for paid work."[1] Accordingly, in his thinking, a woman is inferior because she does not bring in any money, which explains why some men, who are part of the finance teams in some church circuits, only want to pay their male pastors. These men believe that women are destined only for obedience to men and procreation by men. For women in pastoral positions, we find that some members are overly aggressive and seek to intimidate and

---

1   Leonardo Pinheiro, *O Patriarcado do Presente na Contemporanei-dade: Contexto de Violência* (Florianopolis: n.p., 2008), 2.

bully the female pastor in order to get their way, which might not be God's way for the church. Ideas brought to the congregation by a female pastor for the development of Christian community are devalued. However, despite these obstacles, women can exercise their dignity, competence, professional identity, and skill to overcome all barriers that hinder the church's faith development.

Despite patriarchal thinking, not all women agreed to be inferior in biblical culture. Despite patriarchal thinking, not all women in southern Mozambique, particularly those in pastoral ministry, believe that women are inferior. And just as we saw women leaders in Bible times, we see women leaders today. We can also see leadership opportunities that The United Methodist Church in Mozambique affords women. Beginning in 1975 Rev. Amina Isaías was called by God. She was inspired during the Pentecost service and began her formation at the Cambine Theological Seminary for three years. After her graduation in 1979, she was the first woman ordained as an itinerant deaconess for the Cambine parish.

Today the United Methodist Church in Mozambique has more than ninety-four pastors, who minister in the various areas of pastoral ministry. In 2008, a fifty-one-year-old-woman pastor, Joaquina Filipe Nhanala, was elected bishop of the Church in Mozambique, and she succeeded Bishop João Somane Machado at the Central Conference in Mutare, Zimbabwe. Bishop Nhanala is married to Pastor Eugênio Tomás, with whom she has four children. She was ordained a deaconess in 1989 and earned a bachelor's degree in 1995. In 1998 she was awarded a postgraduate degree in Bible Studies from Nairobi College, where she also served as a teacher. As bishop, she leads the North, South, and Southeast (experimental area) of the Mozambique conference, Madagascar, South Africa, and Swaziland. From the beginning of her election, she has faced many leadership challenges, including lack of water holes in the religious communities, particularly in the districts of Morrumbene, Massinga, Vilanculos, Homoine, and in some districts of Gaza province.

In 2011 the sixteen overseers, who led sixteen ecclesiastical districts of the South Mozambique conference, decreased to six and to six corresponding ecclesiastical areas. Then in 2018 the conference added an additional oversight area, making a total of seven. These are currently led by four men and three women. Furthermore, in 2018, South conference was divided into two; namely, the Southeast, as an experimental conference area, and South conference. Women were appointed to prominent areas, such as Rev. Hortência Langa who was appointed to the annual conference DICOM. In her leadership the Bishop Nhanala created an evangelization movement in Madagascar furthering the mission and ministry of The United Methodist Church.

The Role of Women in Government

With the introduction of a political multiparty system, "women have been given greater access to power, as part of a democratic logic with a globalizing character and where there is a struggle for the emancipation of women."[2] Consequently, Mozambican law places men and women in a space of gender equality. According to Agy (2018) this principle of equality was consolidated in the Constitution of the Republic of 1990 and 2004, specifically Articles 67 and 36, which stipulate that men and women are

2   Conceicao Osório, *Political power and female activism* (n. p.), 3. Available from https://www.ces.uc.pt/emancipa/research/pt/ft/mulheres .html. Accessed 5/11/2019.

equal before the law in all areas of political, economic, social, and cultural life.[3] From this decree, and with the signing of a peace agreement in Mozambique, women now have decision-making opportunities. According to Karberg (2015), "women in Mozambique inherited a strong role resulting from the country's liberation struggle, followed by the democratization process."[4] In this regard, Mozambican women have occupied prominent places in society, occupying positions in the political arena such as governors, ministers, and administrators. As a result, most of the missions that the government has entrusted to women have been attended to with great dedication. Women prioritize missions that have been entrusted to them, and they assume their responsibilities with honesty and clear standards of professional ethics for the benefit of all.

According to Osorio (n.d), the struggle for women's equality must take place within the framework of a political organization, because only by banding together can their emancipation expectations be met. The struggle for equality continues, because the ideals of a male-dominated party persist as do seeming preferences for male leadership and practices that are totalitarian and that exclude difference.[5] Moreover, Mozambique is dominated by men's hold on power, such that women's decision-making is seldom heard in the political or religious spheres. This is collaborated by Osório (2010) and Conceição (2013, cited by Karberg, 2015), who say that the strong affiliation is necessary, given women's lack of validation.

---

3   Aleia Rachine Agy, *Gender Inequality in Rural Contexts in Mozambique: Case Study in Nampula Province* (n.p., 2018), 370.

4   Sindy Karberg, *Women's political participation and their influence on empowering women in Mozambique* (n.p.: Friedrich Ebert Stiftung, 2015).

5   Osorio, *Political Power.*

Female Education

In Mozambique education is the right and duty of every citizen.[6] For economic and social development to happen in the country, people need to embrace education. "Education is the main road to preparing the human resources needed for a country's growth and development."[7] In the past, male children were given priority in education because they were considered the heirs in the family. As a result, boys had the right to attend rudimentary education up to the fourth grade, and "seminars were a strong attraction for young Mozambicans because they represented the only possibility for them to continue their studies after primary school."[8] Being in a patriarchal society, girls' instruction only allowed for obedience and procreation in order to become good wives and mothers. Girls who were not yet married were duty-bound to look after their younger siblings and to do all the housework. It is no surprise then that girls' education lagged behind boys, since the family saw no reason to send them to school so they could learn to write and read. It was thought that reading was unimportant and not needed to keep women submissive and as good examples of morals and customs. With the emergence of the democratization process in Mozambique, however, women began to gain space in society at-large. As a result, some women were admitted to theological seminaries and became pastors. In addition, we find Bishop Nhanala increasingly committed to the ongoing formation of pastors for higher education in various areas of education.

---

6   Constitution of the Republic of Mozambique, article 88.
7   Lavinia Gasperini, *Mozambique: education and rural development* (n.p., 1989), 4.
8   Gasperini, 18.

Violence toward Women

Aristotle, as referenced by Santigoi and Coelhoii, defines violence as "everything that comes from outside and opposes the exterior movement of a moral agent; it refers to the physical constraint in which one is obliged to do what he or she does not want (external imposition against absolute interiority and free will)."[9] The English word *violence* come from the word *violentis*, which means "abuse of force," or to transgress the respect due to a person (Marcondes Filho, 2001). Violence, as I see it, is a physical, moral, or psychological transgression of one person against another. With this definition in mind, it is clear that in the patrilineal culture in southern Mozambique there is systematic and culturally sanctioned violence against women. This society urges parents, for economic reasons, to force their daughters into early marriage, sometimes to men much older than themselves. Forcing girls to marry before they have the desire or are fully capable of deciding for themselves to marry, violates their rights and can set them up for psychological and physical abuse by denying them the opportunity to be all that God intends as valuable people of God.

Conclusion

Because the southern region of Mozambique is patrilineal and dominated by patriarchal culture, it follows that women, even leaders in parish ministry, are looked down upon by patriarchs in the family, Church, and government and seen only as able to provide care in the domestic sphere. It is true that a woman is

---

9   Rosilene Santiagoi and Coelhoii Maria, *Violence Against Women: Historical Background* (n.p., n.d).

extremely important in child-rearing and property management and often assumes the role of boss in the absence of her husband when he goes to seek employment in South Africa or elsewhere. So, even in this culture, women are seen as capable if only to a limited degree. Yet, even in the sectors where she is begrudgingly given leadership, her decision-making is second-guessed and often rejected. While education has been beneficial for the rights of women, women are still underrepresented.

Yet, at the same time, the Church has the responsibility to teach from the text and show that there are women leaders in the Bible. And the Church has the opportunity to live into its God-given call to be a community of faithful disciples of Jesus when all are treated with justice, fairness, and equity.

FIVE

A Study of *Ewa*

A Focusing on the Theory of Intersectionality

Hyun Ju Lee, PhD

The theory of intersectionality, which was developed first by legal scholar Kimberle W. Crenshaw, is one of the most influential feminist theories in the twenty-first century. While the early stage of the development of Crenshaw's theory focused on the racial and gender prejudices of white men, the word *intersectionality* has now become a key word and concept for understanding and analyzing the racial, gender, and class discriminations against black women and even other women of color.

Ewa: A Tale of Korea was written by William Arthur Noble in 1906, so it would seem to be difficult to apply the theory of intersectionality to this novel. But analyzing this novel from the intersectional perspective can be a new way for understanding the racial, gender, and class discriminations of a white American male missionary in Korea such as William Arthur Noble. This chapter examines white male missionaries' prejudices against Asian women through the male and female characters presented in *Ewa: A Tale of Korea*. Then I analyze the different points of view of Asian women between male and female missionaries in the 1990s with comparison to *Daybreak in Korea* (1909), a novel written by an American female missionary in Korea, Annie Laurie Baird, who had deep sympathy for poor Asian women.

Intersectionality Theory

Kimberle W. Crenshaw, an American lawyer, civil rights activist, and full-time professor at the UCLA School of Law and Columbia Law School, is the first legal scholar who developed the theory of intersectionality. In her article "Demarginalizing the Intersection of Race and Sex: A Black Feminist Critique of Antidiscrimination Doctrine, Feminist Theory and Antiracial Politics" (1989),[1] Crenshaw raised her voice about the racial and gender prejudices of the white men and women who did not regard black women as humans with equal rights. By analyzing three legal cases that discriminated against black women, Crenshaw studied the miserable condition of black women focusing upon the word *intersectionality*.

Since the early stage of the development of Crenshaw's theory of intersectionality, the term has become a key concept for understanding and analyzing racial, gender, and class discrimination against black women and even other women of color. Nevertheless, Crenshaw is not the first womanist scholar who criticized white males' and females' racial and gender

---

1   Kimberle Williams Crenshaw, "Demarginalizing the Intersection of Race and Sex: A Black Feminist Critique of Antidiscrimination Doctrine, Feminist Theory and Antiracist Politics," *University of Chicago Legal Forum* 1989, no. 1, art. 8: 139–67.

discrimination against black and other women of color. A Greek political feminist scholar, Anna Carastathis, wrote, "Women-of-color feminism cannot *but* have succeeded a prior, originally (if admittedly flawed) white feminism, which is dated to the nineteenth century."[2]

Background and Context

Ewa: A Tale of Korea was written in 1906 by Arthur Noble, an American missionary to Korea. The title implies that the plot of this novel is developed around the main female character. However, the plot of this novel is actually the main male character's journey of finding his identity as a Christian leader. Throughout the novel, the writer does show the white man's patriarchal gender prejudices against Asian women and their ways of life. This chapter will try to find the presence and evidence of these prejudices, focusing on the theory of intersectionality.

The year 1892, when William Arthur Noble (1866-1941), an American missionary of Methodist Episcopal Church, published *Ewa*, belongs to the period when the political and moral canon of Korea's Joseon Dynasty (1392-1897) was still dominated strongly by Confucianism. Confucianism, which emphasized the strict patriarchism, had a great influence on family relations and even customs during the Joseon Dynasty as shown in the following sentences written by an anonymous missionary:

> While Confucianism exalts filial piety to the position of the highest virtue, and while a Confucianist makes this very common principle hide a multitude of uncommon sins, the

---

2 Anna Carastathis, *Intersectionality: Origins, Contestations, Horizons* (Lincoln & London: University of Nebraska Press, 2016), 25.

whole system saps the foundation of morality and prosperity by classifying women with menials and slaves. When, a year after the death of the expelled wife of Confucius, his son wept over her loss, the great sage was offended, because it was improper that a son should so long mourn over his mother's death, while the father still lived! A woman, in the Confucian morality, is virtuous in proportion as she is dull.[3]

In the Confucian society, males were the only members who could rule and control the family matters, while females had to obey them without question. Expressing any contrary views or opinions against males' suggestions or orders was considered an offense against public or traditional custom. In the case of wives, the traditional family rules were more severe. Wives were required to live as "deaf for three years" and "mute for another three years" after getting married. They could not express their jealousy or anger even when their husbands had many concubines.

The societies of Western European countries and North America in the late nineteenth century were breaking down their patriarchal gates to women, even though the transitions took place slowly. The women who were prevented from having opportunities for higher education, the women who had no political and property rights, and the women whose duties were limited to taking care of their home and family members—those women came out on the streets and raised their voices to gain political rights as well as the opportunity to have higher education. As a result of these strong feminist movements, a lot of Western women came to have the same political, social, and educational rights and opportunities as men had. Nevertheless, the social realities

---

3   Anonymous, "Confucianism in Korea," *The Korean Repository* (November 1895): 402.

they encountered were still harsh. Even though the women in this age had been educated enough to work in professional fields, they still faced difficulties finding jobs in those fields. Therefore, many highly educated Christian women who wanted to pursue their dreams as professionals chose instead to become missionaries to foreign countries, especially those Asian countries such as China, Japan, India, and Korea.[4]

Nevertheless, even in the Asian mission fields where Western female missionaries were doing their mission work, they still could not overcome the limits of patriarchal social systems, especially in the case of married couples. The biggest barrier to doing mission work was the horrible conditions in which to raise babies. Sanitary problems, especially, made mothers hesitate to do mission work outside their homes. Due to this terrible situation, these women could not meet even the basic requirement for starting their mission work, which was to attend Korean language courses. Mrs. Appenzeller, who came to Korea in 1885 with her husband, gave Western female missionaries this advice: "Then what can a woman do? If possible learn the language before you have the care of a house; but if, as in many cases, that is impossible, be sure you do not do harm in your efforts to do good."[5] This advice shows the social reality that female missionaries, especially wives, had to suffer from the traditional social roles given to them while male missionaries had the freedom to move about and attend to their mission work.

---

4   Leslie A. Flemming, "A New Humanity: American Missionaries Ideals for Women in North India, 1870-1930," *Western Women and Imperialism*, ed. Mupur Chaudhui and Margaret Strobel (Bloomington: Indiana University Press, 1992), 193.

5   Ella Dodge Appenzeller, "Mrs. Appenzeller's Address," *The Korean Repository* (November 1895): 421.

When a young engaged couple, William and Mattie, were dispatched to Korea as missionaries, they went to the library and tried to find "everything available on Korea."[6] Unfortunately they couldn't find anything available. In the 1890s, as British explorer and writer Isabella Bird Bishop described, Korea was just one of the mysterious, unknown countries that Western people were curious about.

> In the winter of 1894, when I was about to sail for Korea (to which some people erroneously give the name of "The Korea"), many interested friends hazarded guesses at its position—the Equator, the Mediterranean, and the Black Sea being among them, a hazy notion that it is in the Greek Archipelago cropping up frequently. It was curious that not one of these educated, and, in some cases, intelligent people came within 2,000 miles of its actual latitude and longitude![7]

Without having any information available in Korea, the American missionary couple still had to face a strong patriarchal society. In this society the American white male missionary had few chances to meet Korean women of high or middle classes, because they were prohibited from walking outside of their homes except in some special cases.[8] The only females that the American white missionary could see were *Gi-saengs* (Korean geishas), slaves, and the lower-class women. While watching their miserable lives, the American white male missionary felt pity. However, he probably understood them only from a limited

---

6 Wilcox A. Nobel, "Our Arrival in Seoul," *The Korea Mission Field* (August 1930), 160.

7 Isabella Bird Bishop, *Korea and Her Neighbours* (Seoul: Yonsei University Press, 1970), 11.

8 James F. Lee, "Magnificient Personality: Korea through the Eyes of Western Women," *Korean Culture* 14, no. 1 (Spring 1993): 34.

point of view that stereotyped gender prejudices like other intelligent white men. In his eyes a *Gi-saeng* seemed to be simply a smiling sexual puppet who had no serious consciousness about herself and the war as a human.

> But the gaudy plaything of the rich and idle—the professional dancing girl—remained. Grim war has no terrors for her, the fierce hand of hate grows soft and gracious under her wanton smile. They were at the feast in paint and silks, like gaudy butterflies, not to partake of the feast, but to nestle near with why glances, giving the occasion a sense of voluptuousness and luxury.[9]

Actually, most of *Gi-saengs* were from extremely poor families. As Annie Baird, the American Presbyterian missionary, described in her novel *Daybreak in Korea: A Tale of Transformation in the Far East* (1909), they were sold to the official governments or private *Gi-saeng* houses by their parents when they were children. Some girls who escaped came back home and begged for their parents to open the door, but their parents did not accept them and even pushed them out, ordering them to go back to the *Gi-saeng* house.

> In a lighted doorway Pobai saw a little girl no older than herself whom she knew very well. It was Shining Peachblossom. . . . Now she was back again, and Pobai saw that she was panting as if she had been running. Her face looked very wan and thin and unchildlike under the powder and paint, and Pobai heard her say: "Oh, if you'll just let me stay quietly at home, mother, you don't know how hard I will work. It's dreadful down where

---

9   Arthur Noble, *Ewa: A Tale of Korea* (New York: Eaton & Mains, 1906), 160.

I am. I'm afraid, I'm afraid!" Pobai did not hear the answer, but presently there was the sound of push, a little cry, the slam of a door, and looking back, she saw Shining Peachblossom fallen a little crumpled heap by the side of the path.[10]

The reason why they smiled and danced was that it was *Gi-saeng*'s way. If they protested or rejected their duty, it meant they would give up their living, even their life.

Ewa

I begin with a minor female character in *Ewa*. She is the daughter of Mr. Yi, a nouveau riche. Even though Mr. Yi earned a lot of money through trade and lives like *Yang-bans* (the aristocrats), he cannot be treated as aristocratic because he was originally from a lower-class family. In the story his daughter is engaged to marry Sung-yo, the main male character, but he deserts her because of her appearance.

> I placed my eye to the hole, but at first I could see only the outline of a woman sitting on the floor near the candle, who seemed to be bending over engaged in folding a garment that was lying at her feet. I looked till she turned her face full into the light which flared up at that moment revealing a face in which I could not see a trace of intelligence, and the impression of a stooping attitude that I had at first observed was caused by a deformed body. She presently stood up by the candlelight, a hunchback, short and ugly.[11]

---

10 Annie Baird, *Daybreak in Korea: A Tale of Transformation in the Far East* (New York: Fleming H. Revell Company, 1909), 16.

11 Noble, *Ewa*, 70.

The author does not explain the reasons why she has to be criticized as a dull person. There is no explanation why the male character's broken engagement is justified either. If we manage to find any reason for the justification of his desertion, it is her appearance. She is only a short, ugly hunchback.

The main female character, Ewa, however, is described as the opposite of the daughter of Mr. Yi.

> The contrast of her person, with the deformed creature that had been chosen for my bride, made her appear exceedingly fair. The face was long, rather than round, eyes large, but of what color I could not tell. They did not flinch before one's glance and seemed always to carry the impression of wondering interest. The lips were firm and gave her an expression of steady trustworthiness and the power to endure. When she smiled, all the sunshine of a sweet nature came into her face, robbing, I thought, the flowers by the wayside of their brightness.[12]

Ewa is a daughter from a Yang-ban family, but Mr. Yi conspires against her family because he wants to have Ewa's mother as his concubine. Consequently, Ewa and her mother run away in order to escape their situation in which they had to live as slaves. Just after her mother passes away on the road, Ewa returns to Mr. Yi and offers herself to him to satisfy his need for revenge. Under the circumstances where slaves had to obey whatever their owners ordered, Ewa makes all efforts to keep her virginity. However, these efforts prompt serious persecution by Mr. Yi. There are many times when she is beaten nearly to death. As a result of her strong

---

12 Noble, 132-3.

protests, Mr. Yi finally gives up forcing her to sleep with him. Instead, he attempts another strategy, to allure her to be his concubine.

The author tells us that Ewa could have lived a comfortable life if she had accepted Mr. Yi's offer to be his concubine. However, she protests and rejects his offer, and she instead chooses Sung-yo as her husband. Because she is a Christian, she evangelizes Sung-yo, and they get married among Christians in a small, secret church. Without having the first night with her husband, Ewa returns to Mr. Yi, because she believes that Christians should be examples to the world. She pledges to be Mr. Yi's slave of her own will, and she believes that her owner should know about her marriage. She asks Mr. Yi for forgiveness and mercy because she got married without permission. However, his jealousy and anger lead to her death.

Interpretation

Ewa was written for American Methodists. Its main goal was to chronicle the importance of Christian evangelization of Korea by American missionaries.[13] It was probably not Noble's intention to portray the realities of gender and class discrimination against women. The writer's focus is on how the main male character, Sung-yo, goes from being an ordinary person to a Christian leader. But Noble does show gender prejudice in that Korean women, especially *Gi-saengs* and females of the lower class, have no intelligence. He considers *Gi-saengs* as just wanton females who have no interest in national, political, or social

---

13 Hyaeweol Choi, "(En)Gendering a New Nation in Missionary Discourse: An Analysis of W. Arthur Noble's *Ewa,*" *Korea Journal* (Spring 2006): 142.

circumstances. This extends even to the daughter of a nouveau riche man. The author describes her only as an ugly woman who has no intelligence even though her deformed and ugly body symbolize her father's distorted desire for the rise of social status.

The life of a main male character betrays Noble's biased thought that women cannot be leaders. As Dong-sik, another Christian guide for Sung-yo's spiritual growth, says, "The land is full of men that needed to be bolstered up by women. There are many who have little more vigor than an oyster, and the vision of a strong woman would put them to flight."[14] Ewa is only a "virgin wife,"[15] who invites and leads Sung-yo into the journey of finding himself. Contrary to the other female characters in the novel, Ewa stands against her miserable destiny. It is Ewa who returns to Mr. Yi and becomes his slave. It is Ewa who chooses to be a Christian and marry Sung-yo. Nevertheless, what is waiting for her courageous and self-directed choices and actions is the death by fatal beatings. In the eyes of a white male missionary, only a man who comes from a noble family can be a Christian leader. Even a woman who comes from a far nobler family cannot be a Christian leader.

Noble is respected as a missionary who had great sympathy for Koreans. It is true that he devoted his whole life to the evangelization and enlightenment of Korean people. Some scholars who study Korean Christian history might think that it is inadequate to analyze Noble just from the view of intersectionality theory. Others might say that to understand Noble as a white man with racial, gender, and class prejudices toward Korean women underestimates his merits. Nevertheless, this analysis can be a meaningful approach to broaden our understanding of foreign missionaries in the beginning of the twentieth century.

---

14 Noble, *Ewa*, 197-8.
15 Noble, 308.

SIX

Breaking the Spell of Patriarchy and Ushering in God's Reign

A Postcolonial Reading of Patriarchy

MEMORY CHIKOSI, MA

Zimbabwe is a patriarchal country where men have power over women. Women have long been marginalized by men's cultural attitudes and actions. Gender inequality is even manifest in the lifestyle of churchmen, so that local churches consequently reflect patriarchal society rather than God's intended future for the community of faith. Likewise, trouble related to gender discrimination is a reality in the Zimbabwe Episcopal Area of The United Methodist Church (ZEACUMC). Despite the fact that women are the majority in the church, its top leadership is dominated by men, because some conservatives resist gender equality even though some progressives support it.

Despite the fact that some male pastors and lay preachers adopt the idea of equality of men and women, the majority still adhere to traditional religious notions about male authority. Men think that male dominance is hereditary and therefore inevitable, thus their sermons teach that a Christian woman belongs in the home, even as they entertain the fantasy that women want to obey men without question. Men discourage women's independence and insist that only serving the family is service to God. They dispirit women from resisting patriarchal bondage, even when they know that there are women who surpass them in education and leadership skills.

Furthermore, these male preachers use their influence and authority to support and maintain cultural notions of masculinity and promote patriarchy as normative for Christians. This power imbalance of men over women brought about by years of cultural tradition and religious teaching makes women vulnerable to neglect and abuse in their homes and in society more generally. In addition, conservative male attitudes and beliefs are barriers to healthy church growth; however, women's partnership with supportive men can challenge abusive traditional values. This chapter examines gender inequality, attempting to address neocolonialism, which in this case means the continuation of women's exploitation. Using religious and cultural pressure to control and influence women and keep them merely as men's dependents only benefits entrenched and unjust patriarchal power even in the Church. Last, this chapter proposes that the Church enforce its endorsement of gender equality norms in faith communities to protect women from abuse.

Patriarchy and the Origin of Gender Discrimination

Gender inequality has been in existence since ancient times. In the Old and New Testaments' patriarchal context, women were regarded as incapable of even giving legal testimony and barred from participating in some religious rites and reading the Torah. This was due to the myth that only men were acceptable images of God. Francis Machingura comments that the Torah describes women as caregivers and household managers but that women and children did not even attend temple services.[1] Society was controlled by men, and women were largely excluded from any real decision-making, especially in the political and public spheres. This inequality gave and is still giving men advantages in the Church, making the Church culpable in promoting women's involuntary subordination.

However, there is no specific evidence from archaeology concerning the individual daily lives of biblical patriarchs such as Abraham, Isaac, and Jacob. The Genesis 12-50 narratives about the origins of the Hebrew people including the patriarchs are primarily theological not historical. There are no archaeological findings to corroborate their beliefs and circumstances. The Old Testament presents the patriarchal narratives as a series of origin narratives and myths (Genesis 1-11), beginning with creation and extending to the lives of the patriarchs, including genealogies from Adam to Abraham.[2] Accordingly, whether or not the historical facts concerning patriarchal traditions are discernable, why should the Church be held hostage to its past? Why didn't the biblical writers provide matriarchal narratives in these origin stories? Were there no matriarchs who partnered with patriarchs? This begs the question: Was the patriarchal system reflected in the Bible created by God, or was it a human creation? Whatever the reason that women are portrayed in the Bible as they are, we can only say that it impacts relationships between men and women today.

---

1   Francis Machingura, "A Diet of Wives as a Lifestyle of Vapositiri Sects: The Polygamy Debate in the Face of HIV and AIDS in Zimbabwe," *Africana* 5, no. 2 (2011): 185-210.

2   Laymon, 1971.

Biblical Perspectives of Womanhood and Manhood

In the Bible, men and women complement each other to varying degrees. It is not God's design that men and women contest, push, critize, and cast off each other. Manhood and womanhood are meant to be mutually interrelated. We all recognize that human life is a creation of God, not a commodity to be exploited. Hence, men and women must be united in faith communities on an equal footing, treating each other with respect. They must create a robust working relationship in all church life including worship. While men and women need to recognize their differences and the fact that they may operate with different sets of rules and expectations, there is no excuse for men to dominate women. Both genders need to acknowledge and value each other's uniqueness. Let us celebrate our differences, realizing that we are both made in the same image of God (Gen 1:26-27).

Complementing and valuing one another's uniqueness is a mature position. Both should avoid seeing differences in others as weaknesses, disorders, or bad or stupid. Women and men are capable of understanding each other and of worshipping together without threatening each other. Seeing each other as God intended will bring harmony to the Church.[3]

Gendered Discourses in Church Communities

One Sunday morning at a worship service, I heard a male pastor preach on God's grace using Genesis 12:14-16 as his text. In this sermon he said that God favored and saved Abraham from harm

---

3 Mark Gungor, *Laugh Your Way to a Better Marriage: Unlocking the Secrets to Life, Love, and Marriage* (RSA: Christian Art Publishers, 2017), 29-31.

because he surrendered his wife to Pharaoh as his sister. Here, the preacher only thought of Abraham's safety, not realizing that Sarah was at risk in the hands of Abraham's opponents. Even if Sarah was Abraham's sister, would it be right to surrender one's sister to abusers in order to save one's life? We can ask, How was that sermon heard by women? I know I felt devalued as a woman. Would my safety not matter to this preacher? Would any woman's?

Furthermore, during a United Theological College (UTC) fourth-year internship seminar, a male student gave the closing devotion in which he said, "As a thoughtful preacher and knowing that the day has been busy, I will not be long, but brief like a mini-skirt covering the subject." This is a typical statement that uses lewd gender imagery to carry a clear intention to demean women. Another male student shared his ministry experience by saying, "Feminists trying to run things is a problem at my church." He went on to describe one female leader in his parish as dominating, disrespectful, arrogant, and loud in administrative council meetings. This statement indicates that some male pastors do not know what to do with women leaders who have strong personalities—women who are able to confront situations head-on or push back against male authority. In such cases, men must confess their need for help, own their weakness, appreciate women with administration skills, and stop blaming and undercutting women. Also, male pastors should learn to differentiate administrative from feminist issues.

Another male lecturer who was presenting on the topic of bereavement counseling said, "In counseling sessions, women fail to express their feelings when they say things like, 'I want to remarry,' when they have lost a loved one. They can be very emotional when they are failing to have sex." Aside from being shocked that grief counseling has been reduced in such a way, the whole presentation centered on women's need for counseling, as if women are the only ones who mourn the loss of a spouse. Moreover, these typical generalizations betray negative opinions about women. Although at the beginning the presenter indicated that he supports women, his presentation displayed male bias. Then, during an open discussion on gender violence at UTC, it was generally agreed that women and the girls are disproportionately affected by gender violence, although some men are also victims and need help.

Again, a student preaching in the UTC Chapel on 1 Timothy 2:12 said: "But I suffer not a woman to teach nor to usurp authority over the man; but to be in silence."[4] He went on to declare that "sometimes women forget their lower status before they got married." The whole sermon was addressed to women as if there were no men in the pews. Another male preached on Ephesians 5:22-24 and said, "The text shows that in the beginning God did not speak to women." This misreading and misunderstanding of the Bible aligns with Storkey's suggestion that men read and preach from the Bible selectively and in line with their prejudice against women; thus they misinterpret Scripture and consequently come up with policies that negate and demoralize women.[5]

In a discussion group composed of fifteen women at UTC, the conversation centered on the fact that most women are isolated and silenced by sermons that use texts such as Ephesians 5:22, which says: "Wives, submit yourselves unto your own husbands,

---

4   Frank Charles Thompson, DD, ed., The Thompson Chain-Reference Bible (5th improved ed.): King James Version (Cambridge: Cambridge University Press, 1988), 1261.

5   Elaine Storkey, *What's Right with Feminism* (London: SPCK, 1985), 35.

as unto the Lord."[6] When women have been sexually abused, these sermons make them recall their traumatic experiences, which is especially tragic when women still suffer abuse and can even smell the abuser. The shame and guilt are so pervasive that these women keep to themselves, making it difficult for them to enter into the community fellowship that churches offer, thus stifling opportunities for spiritual growth.

Determining Factors and the Effect of Gender Discrimination

Humanity's view of manhood and womanhood is that both males and females have been created in the likeness of God but as distinguished beings. Those in power then use their gender to create politics and politics to construct and control gender. This social construction is so taken for granted that the depth of bias and prejudice are not noticed in a conscious way. Gender bias, prejudice, and privilege become simply the way things are—tradition—and, by extension, the way they should be. This means that those who are deemed less powerful (women) are given less access to needed information that could afford them greater protection, while at the same time putting them at increased risk for abuse. Downplaying women's difficulties and heightening men's difficulties leads to unrealistic expectations, while also depriving women of finding new ways to advance themselves through education and good high-paying jobs, especially given their social isolation. If women only see traditional avenues open to them, they will confine themselves strictly to domestic roles, depriving the larger society and market square of their intelligence and ingenuity.

---

6   Thompson, Thompson Chain Reference Bible, KJV, 1244.

Although the Church has empowered some women, nevertheless they are assigned to lower leadership positions. When women show high potential for Church ministry, men view them in a pejorative light and lump them together as radical feminists, those who want to overthrow men from leadership positions. Consequently, women who aspire to occupy higher leadership positions face resistance and are sabotaged. They are considered unethical and even immoral, such that women in the Church are threatened by them, and they fear that these strong women will want to take their husbands and break up their marriages. Therefore, when leadership selection time comes, women do not choose other women but look to men, because they have bought the leadership myth that leadership posts are for men only.

As a result, male control endures as a reality in Church leadership. Therefore, Russell and Clarkson say, "The degree to which an institution is gendered is reflected in the extent to which it is led by one gender."[7] At present in Zimbabwe there is only one female bishop in The United Methodist Church from among all the female alumnae of the affiliate Churches of United Theological College. The UMC has entrusted authority to women as district superintendents, but the position of bishop has never been offered to a female. The Church then mirrors the larger society that says women cannot lead as bishops, even if they are as capable as men.

Patriarchy and Women in the Church

In Africa, Church spirituality as expressed in its concerns for the security of women is still governed by the demands of traditional

---

7   Letty M. Russell and J. Shannon Clarkson, eds., *Dictionary of Feminist Theology* (Westminster: Crossroads, 1996), 126.

cultures, which go against Jesus's ethics. Yet women remain in solidarity with the Church as they look forward, even when the Church takes them for granted and unjustly preserves male power. Thus, a transformation of the world's patriarchal values and practices to one of justice and safety is needed. But, on the other hand, the Church's leadership has helped discontinue discourses against women by supporting women's emancipation through organizing women and youth seminars in communities. The Church has also increased the awareness of gender discrimination and encouraged women to be unwavering in their quest for full rights and representation in the Church and civil society. Because the Church has the mandate to guard and promote human dignity, leadership must be pious and lead a holistic Christian life in order to show kingdom values that support peace and reconciliation, compassion and justice for men and women.

The ZEACMUMC as a nurturing community is called to lead the way to gender equality because it affirms gender diversity.[8] It therefore should:

- help men observe Wesleyan Christian social ethics;
- develop Christian relief campaigns to help sufferers from patriarchal oppression;
- work with government and other supportive agencies to fight discriminatory standards that make a male abusive culture friendlier toward women;
- revise its vision and mission statements and make sure they are aligned to the desired goal of reconciling both genders;

---

8   "The United Methodist Social Principles: Working Draft 1": The UMC General Board of Church and Society, April 11, 2018, p. 11, https://ntcumc.org/English_Draft_of_the_Revised_Social_Principles.pdf.

- develop a gender-friendly Church culture that allows both genders to move, worship, and live freely and comfortably;
- transform structures and functions in ways that women own and contribute to worship spaces[9];
- support interreligious women associations that promote policies that deter women from full participation;
- use holistic practical approaches to embrace both genders as people made in God's image.

Pastors and Church leaders at local levels should:

- spearhead gender equity by valuing similarities and differences of both gender roles;
- promote and support both genders without bias so as to ensure fairness and strengthen the relationship connection of its members;
- assign sermon passages and encourage preachers to be more intentional about their sermons and how they will be heard by both genders;
- preach and teach on gender reconciliation from the pulpit[10];
- refrain from statements that impinge unfairly on women;
- help both genders accept and respect each other;
- help women showcase their potential and distinctiveness; and
- help women rise up when they fall in their journey alongside of men.

---

9 H. Jurgens Hendriks et al., *Men in the Pulpit, Women in the Pew?* (Stellenbosch: Sun Press, 2010).

10 M. Baden, *Gender Discrimination* (Geneva: WCC Publications, 2000).

Doing these things will help promote gender sensitivity both in the Church and in the broader society. It will also help to compensate for the historical and social disadvantages that prevent women from worshipping, moving to, and functioning in their full potential in the Church.[11]

Policies

All members should practice gender equity in order for both genders to realize their full human rights and contribute to and benefit from social, cultural, and religious development. Men must recognize that women also use reason and sacrifice. They can be helpful, patient, and industrious; instruments of peace, health, and mercy. They can be soft yet strong, attentive mothers. They can be leaders of families, churches, and societies. They can be friends, advisors, and educators of men, and they are expressions of humanity in general. We cannot talk about churches without mentioning women, but how often are women hurt by male insensitivity? Constantly dealing with and experiencing hurt makes women doubt their worthiness and their value to the Church and to God. Consequently, men should replace a deconstructive theory[12] with the reconstructive theory, reconcile with women, help them deal with the hurt they have experienced, and construct new healthier families and church communities where women can have opportunities to lead, protect, and love. Therefore men must:

---

11 R. Gatti, *Church Development and Gender Issues* (Roma, Nuova, Arnica: Denver Publications, 1999), 27.

12 John Mullarkey and Beth Lord, eds., *The Continuum Companion to Continental Philosophy* (London and New York: Continuum Books, 2009).

- appreciate the femininity of women and see them as human beings and bearers of God's image;
- not use male-female differences to handicap or ostracize women for who they are;
- treat women as equals in terms of influence in religious, moral issues and opportunities;
- be sensitive and aware of women's needs and interests;
- take Jesus and Paul (who overcame limitations of their contexts and tradition by welcoming Gentiles, Jews, women, and men) as models (Mark 7:24-30; Gal 3:38);
- realize that Jesus's ministry was supported by both men and women; and
- not deny women opportunities for self-discovery.

If a just world is to be realized, women should reject patriarchy as part of the natural order. They should help each other realize their potential to become prominent people who transcend and transform social, cultural, and religious hierarchies. Women should confront their imposed status as permanently marginalized people and challenge men to respect all women whatever their age, color, and social status. Men and women must allow women space to occupy positions of power without fear of repercussions that seek to shame, humiliate, and exclude them as leaders and relegate them to only being wives and mothers. Women must:

- uphold and appreciate the maleness of men and their own femininity to avoid skirmishes and heartbreak;
- be self-determined, courageous, and willing to support each other in fighting patriarchy and the structural inequalities that men use as weapons to degrade women;
- reclaim their lost God-given gift of power for their liberation and for the whole human race;

- report ill-treatment against them;
- strive to open traditional church hierarchies so that they can participate in and increase women's representation on church boards and in the public sphere;
- set their own agendas, gain skills, build self-confidence, develop self-reliance, and stop waiting for men to solve their problems;
- look for international cooperation agencies to support their self-empowerment programs;[13]
- learn to say no to men's decisions that do not support women's causes;
- be inspired by and knowledgeable about prominent women in the Bible such as Mary, Martha, Priscilla, Chloe, and Phoebe;
- not allow men to deny them the freedom to worship and be worship leaders; and
- reproach women who collaborate with male power to ensure the continuity of men's interests at the expense of women's interest.

Conclusion

The elimination of patriarchy needs the cooperation of women and men. Seeing women as strong, valuable images of God will help women fulfill their full potential in the family, workplace, Church, and society. It will benefit all people—men, women, and children. The spell of patriarchy exploits all people, and especially women; but it can be broken so that we together, women and men, can usher in a new era and bring us all closer to God's reign.

---

13 Gatti, *Church Development*.

SEVEN

Mutual Partnership

Negotiating Patriarchal Structures in Vietnam

QUYNH-HOA NGUYEN, PhD

I would like to start with the reality that Vietnamese women, in both church and society, are experiencing today. Asian women's experience, common and diverse, is central for Asian feminist theologians to construct and present their theology.[1] Vietnamese women's experience of subordination and submission will be a focus for my theological reflection.

Recently, the couple who own Vietnam's largest coffee corporation divorced. The judge repeatedly encouraged the wife, who is a successful businesswoman, to turn over the whole company to her husband in order to stay home and take care of the children.

At a particular church wedding, a woman pastor preached on the Ephesians household code, in which she kept calling

---

1   Kwok Pui-lan, *Introducing Asian Feminist Theology*, Introductions in Feminist Theology 4 (Sheffield: Sheffield Academic, 2000), 38-50.

husbands to lead their wives, saying husbands must be the leader in the home. Note that the Vietnamese term "lead" or "leader" is often used in workplace, church, and society rather than in family relationships. It is ironic that in reality wives are often referred to as the "general of the interior" (*nội tướng*), in charge of the inner realm of the household.

At a first meeting of a women's ministry in May, a woman pastor who led an opening devotion used 1 Peter 3:3-6, emphasizing the value of female submission, quiet spirit, and gentleness. In the following training session the women mainly identified their values as being strong, emotional, gentle, loving, hardworking, enduring, and nurturing; caring for family, and being devoted to God, self-sacrificial, and perseverant.

Again, at a meeting, another woman pastor started her speech with an acknowledgment that men do "big work" and women do "small work."

Those events reflect the gender-inequality issues facing women in Vietnam. The reality could be more dynamic than presented, especially in the larger society. Still, subordination, submission, and inferiority mark much of the identity construction of Vietnamese Christian women today. Though Vietnamese society has a strong matriarchal heritage and socialism that embraces both women's liberation and gender equality, patriarchy is still the norm. A woman is supposed to be subordinate to her husband even if she has more potential. Her success is still about having a happy home and successful marriage. Women internalize the traditional values that the patriarchal society attributes to them as "divine calling." In church, even when women pastors are privileged to have voice, still they unconsciously reinforce this mentality. They lift up the household code when women are gathering or when they are experiencing a ritual, instead of engaging with codes of women's discipleship.

I am interested in connecting the experience of Vietnamese Christian women with the patriarchal culture of the Church and the larger society to search for an alternative. I address the cultural and theological issues that underline women's reinforcement of patriarchy. Then I suggest a partnership model that transgresses the traditional male-dominated structures.

Confucianism, with its predominant ideology of patriarchy, has led to submission of women to men, embedded in family and society. Like many other countries in Asia, Vietnam was influenced by Confucianism for centuries. Though the Confucian tradition fell into decline in the early twentieth century when Vietnam came to embrace Western thought, Confucianism still leaves its impact on the current family structure. As a means of establishing harmony and order, Confucianism places a moral and social code on women's behavior widely known as the "Three Obediences" and "Four Virtues." The three obediences are obedience to a woman's father when unmarried, obedience to her husband when married, and obedience to her son when widowed. The four virtues include: household skills, proper appearance, proper speech, and proper conduct. Alongside this teaching, women's inferiority has been widely perpetuated with Confucian-related sayings such as "one son means a fortune, ten daughters mean nothing" (*Nhất nam viết hữu, thập nữ viết vô*); "man dominates, woman is subordinate" (*Nam tôn, nữ ti*); or "daughters are outsiders of the patrilineage" (*nữ nhi, ngoại tộc*).

The challenge is that the Bible does offer texts consistent with those patriarchal teachings. The household code tradition of the New Testament, which stresses the subordination of wives to husbands, slaves to masters, and children to fathers, repeatedly appears in the epistles known as Ephesians (chs. 5–6), Colossians (ch. 3), and 1 Peter (ch. 3). They have become popular texts as Vietnamese preachers commonly engage them to address family relationships. Vietnamese women pastors, in turn, appropriate those texts without being aware that they are conforming to the patriarchal culture that dominates and oppresses women themselves. As a result, women embrace patriarchal values as a constitutive part of their Christian identity. They have been shaped by the culture in which they live and by the Bible they hold as the ultimate authority for meaning and knowledge. Christians might be unconscious of the cultural impact, but they are well aware of the authority of the Bible to which they appeal.

Christian choice of texts, however, reinforces the patriarchal understanding of God and the hierarchical structure of the church. God is understood as a "patriarchal divine male" who created and maintained the domination of men over women.[2] Church in Vietnam has been characterized by male domination and female subordination, which engenders submission, marginalization, and exclusion of the weak and the powerless. The household codes have been used to justify the power relation of dominance and submission and to promote women's subordinate roles as God-given. Imbued with this ideology, women voluntarily take the roles and values that patriarchy imposes on them as the gender norms established by God. Engagement with the household codes has limited rather than enriched the roles of women in family and ministry.

Also, there is a power imbalance in the ways the Ephesians code has been read. The Ephesians household code is often

---

2   Rosemary Radford Ruether, "Sexism and Misogyny in the Christian Tradition: Liberating Alternatives," *Buddhist-Christian Studies* 34 (2014): 87.

preached in an unbalanced way to emphasize submission of the wife. The text uses the analogy of Christ's love for the church to stress the husband's duty to love his wife "just as Christ loved the church and gave himself up for her" (5:25). The text again concludes with an instruction for husband to "love his wife as himself" (v. 33). Yet, how often are men admonished to love their wife as their body and give themselves as Christ loves the church? It is true that preachers, both male and female, hardly balance out their preaching on this passage. Words from the pulpit frequently portray men as heads over their wives, while women are consistently enjoined to be submissive to their husbands. This imbalance in textual engagements and readings exposes the need for an alternative.

Our Christian job is not to engage texts to reinforce Confucianism. The Bible provides alternative texts that enable us to negotiate a model of partnership instead of promoting the male superiority and female submission of the Vietnamese culture. Galatians 3:28, in particular, offers an alternative that calls for equal worth of both men and women. It has been a central text to claim equality in race, class, and gender. Of the three pairs— "Jew or Greek," "slave or free," "male and female"—the last one, "there is no longer male and female," received special interest from scholars. There is a no-power imbalance between men and women in the Galatian text. In Christ there is no longer male and female, which affirms the equal standing of gender roles. Both are treated with equal value in family and ministry.

I am aware that the Galatians text has been interpreted with diverse and even opposing views. Feminists see the text as the baptismal declaration asserting equality and oneness of all baptized believers, thereby advocating the elimination of male domination and female submission in the Christian community.

As Elizabeth Schüssler Fiorenza puts it, Galatians 3:28 "claims that in the Christian community all distinctions of religion, race, class, nationality, and gender are insignificant. All the baptized are equal, they are one in Christ."[3] A patristic interpretation, on the contrary, argues for unity rather than equality in the text. This view advocates that the Galatians text emphasizes the spiritual unity of sexual differences in Christ rather than addresses the social gender roles in this world. Augustine, in particular, wrote, "The difference, whether of peoples or of legal status or of sex, indeed already removed in the unity of faith, remains in this mortal life."[4] Thus, he claims that Galatians 3:28 emphasizes spiritual oneness of men and women but does not remove social distinctions in this earthly life. Similarly, Vietnamese Christians, with a spiritualizing tendency, read verse 28 as a statement of spiritual equality. This crucial verse, therefore, becomes insignificant to social gender roles in family and ministry. In Vietnam, where Christians exist as a minority and marginalized community, women in particular face double marginality as Christians in the society and as women in the patriarchal structure of the Church. This spiritual reading perpetuates Vietnamese women's experience of submission and leaves them subordinate to men.

---

3   Elizabeth Schüssler Fiorenza, *In Memory of Her: A Feminist Theological Reconstruction of Christian Origins* (New York: Crossroad, 1983), 213. For feminist perspectives, see also Adela Yarbro Collins, "No Longer 'Male and Female' (Gal 3:28): Ethics and an Early Christian Baptismal Formula," *Journal of Ethics in Antiquity and Christianity* 1 (2019), accessed October 2, 2019, https://jeac.de/ojs/index.php /jeac/article/view/98.

4   Kari Kloos, "'In Christ there is neither male nor female': Patristic interpretation of Galatians 3:28," in *Papers Presented at the Fourteenth International Conference on Patristic Studies Held in Oxford 2003*, ed. F. Young, M. Edwards and P. Parvis (Dudley, MA: Peeters, 2006), 242.

Diverse readings of the Galatians text, however, show that the text can be read differently, depending on the social locations of the reader. For Vietnamese women it invites a reading that challenges the traditional domination-subordination relationship between men and women.

Galatians 3:28 serves as a textual location in which women affirm their equality with men. Wesley Kort, a literary critic, defines "scripture" as location on the textual field that signifies the implicit or explicit texts of beliefs of individuals and communities. He argues that people have particular textual locations that provide them with resources to act meaningfully in the world.[5] Galatians 3:28 provides women with a language and a theology alternative to the patriarchal texts. In this textual location God is seen as giving worth to both male and female. God gives value to women who are not valued to culture; at the same time, he is not diminishing men's value. God, who says there is no longer male and female, treats both men and women with equal worth. If the patriarchal text upholds the traditional culture that women are less than men and should submit to men who have the power, then verse 28 asserts that husband and wife can be partners instead of the husband being more powerful than his wife. It dismantles the male-dominated household and gives rise to a partnership model that moves toward the sexual balance of honor and role. If Ephesians has been used to preach on male leadership over female submission in the family hierarchy model, Galatians invites a partnership that honors social roles of both men and women in the Church and family structures.

---

5   Wesley A. Kort, *"Take, Read": Scripture, Textuality, and Cultural Practice* (University Park, PA: Pennsylvania State University Press, 1996), 2-3.

Partnership is about mutuality that has not been addressed in the patriarchal reading of the Ephesian text. The Greek verb ὑποτάσσω, translated as "submit" or "subject" to one another, has the closest equivalent of "be willing to accept orders from one another" or "willingly accept what others say you should do."[6] Important to this exhortation is a mutual relationship that the Ephesians text promotes to both husband and wife. As Carolyn Osiek points out, Christian household texts, unlike other household texts in Roman society that focus only on the male figures, address both the superior and the subordinate persons in pairs.[7] Mutuality, supported by the Ephesians exhortation, is foundational to transforming male headship into partnership of husband and wife. Duane R. Bidwell suggests a theology of mutuality that "promotes possibility, mutual influence, negotiation, and a sense of 'we-ness' in a relationship—factors that contribute to the longevity and success of covenant partnerships."[8] Partnership thus fosters mutuality through support, submission, respect, acknowledgment, and empowerment. This model does not suggest men and women behave equally or identically; rather it exhorts them to mutually balance out their roles as well as acknowledges the value of both women's traditional work and men's work. Given the context of Vietnam where patriarchy still persists, especially in regard to family structure, partnership would be a way of being workable for men and women in the ambivalent situation between patriarchal dominance and gender equality.

---

6   Paratext 8, UBS Translator's Handbook, Ephesians 5:21.

7   Carolyn Osiek, "Household Codes," Bible Odyssey, accessed October 20, 2019, https://www.bibleodyssey.org/en/people/related-articles/household-codes.

8   Duane R. Bidwell, *Empowering Couples: A Narrative Approach to Spiritual Care* (Minneapolis: Fortress, 2013), 20.

Importantly, Vietnamese folklore offers an interesting resource for exploring the partnership model in marriage. Folklore, seen as contestation derived from the culture of the subordinate classes, can be used to present a different view of the world to dispute the dominant worldview.[9] As such, Vietnamese folklore expresses women's values and their significant roles in the family in the midst of prevailing Confucianism. Along the image of dominant husband and submissive wife, folklore presents mutuality and equal worth in marriage relationships. As one of the folk sayings goes:

Husband and wife are like a pair of chopsticks.
(*Vợ chồng như đũa có đôi.*)

Chopsticks are common in Vietnam, representing not merely table utensils but a metaphor of a couple relationship. They symbolize a power balance and mutuality as they come in pairs, being matched, each one relying on the other to be functional. As such, they reflect a concept of equality, harmony, and partnership in family as an alternative to dominance and submission. Similarly, other folk sayings and folksongs assert this partnership of mutual dependence, mutual support, and mutual success between husband and wife:

A husband is wise, his wife has embroidered shoes to wear,
A wife is wise, her husband receives reliable consult.
(*Chồng khôn vợ được đi hài, vợ khôn chồng được nhiều bài cậy trông.*)

---

9   Luigi Lombardi Satriani, "Folklore as Culture of Contestation," *Journal of the Folklore Institute* 11 (June–August 1974): 99–121.

Wife with husband is like a dragon with wings;
Husband with wife is like a tree in the jungle.
(*Vợ có chồng như rồng có vây, chồng có vợ như cây có rừng.*)

The husband ploughs, the wife transplants, the buffalo
    harrows.
(*Chồng cày, vợ cấy, con trâu đi bừa.*)

A man's property is his wife's work.
(*Của chồng, công vợ.*)

These folklore references resonate with an English saying, "Behind every successful man is a (great) [sadly, "great" is not in the usual quote] woman." It is commonly acknowledged that a woman plays an important role in her husband's success. Does a man help his wife succeed in return? Vietnamese folklore, in this sense, challenges the patriarchal tradition of male headship and female subjection in the household. It provides a model of partnership with mutuality that helps women escape the unbalanced gender structure in the patriarchal family power relations.

Vietnamese Christian women face patriarchal culture within the Church and the wider society. Gender equality is a state ideology; but it is still a challenged concept in the present reality, especially to Christians in Vietnam. Deeply influenced by male-centered ideology, Christian women themselves appropriate and read the biblical text from a patriarchal perspective and reinforce male-centered theology. With the biblical text, its readers, and the Church as sources for patriarchy, the struggle for equality is going to be a long one. Gender equality, which is usually understood as identical social roles and restricting men's privileges, would be labeled as going against centuries of tradition that persistently keep men's respect in the world. Keeping face is a matter of honor for men, which is critically important in Asian cultures. Partnership, which is rooted in folklore as well as in both the Ephesians patriarchal household tradition and the liberating Galatians text, is a way to negotiate with male dominance. It constructs male-female relations based not on hierarchy but on mutuality that speaks to women's experience of God as liberating and empowering, lifting up and not pulling down. God, who created gender difference, gives equal worth to both male and female. Gender role difference does not mean one is superior or subordinate to the other. Both are called to a mutual partnership. The process has been already taking place as reflected in the biblical text and Vietnamese folklore, particular in this beautiful traditional saying:

> As long as husband and wife mutually submit themselves to each other, they can dry up the ocean (*Thuận vợ thuận chồng, tát biển Đông cũng cạn*).[10]

That is, "If men and women mutually submit to each other, they can do anything."

---

10 The Vietnamese verb *thuận* implies different meanings, depending the context. Here it could be *thuận hoà*, which means "get along," or it could mean *thuận phục*, refering to "submit."

EIGHT

The Intersection of "The Fairy and the Woodcutter," Judges 21, and the Burning Sun Club

Taking Women and Extracting Capital from Their Bodies

YANI YOO, PHD

E ven today in Korean society, where women seem to enjoy freedom and achievements, the sexual and economic taking of women against their will is pervasive.[1] In this chapter we will also think of the way the Church interprets Judges 21, a story of the collective abduction of women and forced marriages. For our purpose we will deal with three stories: "The Fairy and the Woodcutter," the biblical story as recounted in Judges 21, and the 2019 incident of the Burning Sun Club in Seoul, Korea. We

---

1 In 1990, 19.1 percent of girls graduated from high school (25.7 percent of boys); and in 2018, 73.8 percent of them (8 percent higher than boys) entered university. But women's employment (50.9 percent), percentage of women in national parliaments (17 percent) are still low, and the gender salary gap is 34.6 percent. The number of female victims of sexual violence is sixteen times higher than male victims. "Women's Lives Seen through Statistics (Korean)," accessed October 31, 2019, https://blog.naver.com/mogefkorea/221678341598.

will observe how each illuminates the others in terms of taking, controlling, and exploiting women's bodies for profit.

"The Fairy and the Woodcutter" and Taking of Women

"The Fairy and the Woodcutter" is a well-known Korean folktale with which children grow up. Here is a summary:[2]

> There once was a poor woodcutter who lived with his old mother. One day, he helped a deer escape from hunters. As a show of gratitude, the deer informed the woodcutter of a nearby pond where fairies came down from the heavens to bathe every month. The deer said that the woodcutter would be able to marry one of the fairies by hiding her winged clothing. He could then come to the rescue of the stranded fairy. The only provison was to keep everything secret from the fairy until they had at least three children. With these instructions, the woodcutter was successful in taking a fairy as his wife, and they had two children together. One day, the woodcutter was sorry to see that the fairy still missed her home in heaven. He confessed that he hid the winged clothing and then gave it to her. Upon wearing it she held her two children in her arms and returned to the heavens. The distraught woodcutter turned to the help of the deer. The deer taught him to ride in a bucket coming from heaven to draw water from the pond. Following that direction, the woodcutter was able to reach the heavens

2 Adapted from the summary on the Korea.net site: http://www.korea.net/NewsFocus/Culture/view?articleId=120797 (accessed on October 31, 2019).

and joined the fairy and his children. They lived together happily ever after there.

This story has long been read as romantic in which the good deed of the woodcutter was rewarded with the marriage to a beautiful daughter of the heavenly god. The basic frame of the story is steeped in Confucianism (serving the old mother, marrying, and having children); it is also male-centered and about retributive justice.

Only recently has the story been undergoing feminist criticism.[3] From a feminist viewpoint, the story contains male fantasy full of crimes against women: voyeurism, theft, kidnapping, illegal confinement, fraud, rape, unwanted pregnancy (which results in giving birth), raising children, and forced labor. In all of these the fairy remains objectified; her feelings are ignored, and she is nothing but a tool taken and moved about arbitrarily by male desires and needs.

One thing feminism has not considered, however, is the economic interests the woodcutter gets from taking the fairy. For much of its history the story was circulated in a preindustrial society where women were engaged in all kinds of work, including tending the home and children, weaving, and so forth—a gray and tiring life. Jiwon Park (1737-1805), a scholar of the Realist School of Confucianism, judged that women and men had the same ability to work the farm; that is 6,600-9,900 meters per person. For a poor man without land, and only with an old

---

3   For example, in a rewritten story by a group of young women, the woodcutter remains naked, and the deer eats only bitter vegetables for punishment for one thousand days. Guoh, *The Fairy Did Not Put Up with It* (Korean), Wisdomhouse, 2019.

mother, being able to marry served his economic, sexual, social, and cultural interests.

The problem is that this folktale exerts a strong influence on the forming of children's values toward women, and its negative effects continue well into adulthood, given that most Koreans have only a traditional frame for understanding this story. Now let us turn to a similar story in the Bible.

Sexual and Economic Interests behind Kidnapping Women in Judges 21

Judges 21 reports how the Israelites and their leaders abducted women for the remaining six hundred Benjaminite soldiers, who were on the verge of extinction after losing a war. They first destroyed Jabesh-gilead and took four hundred young women and then even more women during the festival at Shiloh. In this story, the voices of women and other victims are mute.

Scholars have dealt with the biblical story from many angles but not from sexual and economic viewpoints.[4] The concern about the extinction of the Benjaminite reflects concern about a decrease of population and, accordingly, weakening of the whole community's economic and political power. Although both "The Fairy and the Woodcutter" and Judges 21 do not mention any profit from taking women, their kidnapping is paramount to the economic interests of the leaders, the Benjaminites, and the whole of Israel.

---

4   See my previous work, "Reading Judges 21 as a Parody: Remembering the Young Women of Jabesh-gilead and Shiloh," in *Sexual Violence, The Bible and the Korean Church*, ed. Jisung Kwon (Seoul: CLC, 2019), 90-116.

Carol Meyers, on the basis of archaeological and anthropological researches, concluded that women in the Iron Age (1,200–1,000 BCE) of ancient Israel made a considerable contribution to the economy.[5] While men provided labor for military, metallurgy, and agriculture works, women took charge of food process and preparation and the allocation of resources. Women also handled subsistence crafts (making clothes, pottery, and tools) and technology allied with the process of perfumery. Overall, women and men living at subsistence level worked complementarily and interdependently. As in most premodern, labor-intensive societies, it was critical to secure survival by drawing on the labor of a large family. Women were necessary as child bearers and caretakers, but they had to be obtained from outside the family and at a price.[6] It was worthwhile to invest in women because, for the rest of their lives, they would benefit the family in many ways. As in some societies, the Israelite marriage law was more concerned with property transmission than with personal or family dynamics. Family was the most important social unit, because it meant survival, as individuals could survive only in communities. The women's abduction in Judges 21 would guarantee these benefits and, at the same time, eliminate paying the bride price.

The tribe of Benjamin was to be saved by hook or by crook. For example, a Korean commentary for preachers interprets the text this way: "Among the inhabitants of Jabesh-gilead, only the young women who did not know men and remained pure were clothed with the grace of salvation." This means that "we need to lead a pure life in order not to be destroyed with this world, but

---

5   Carol Meyers, *Discovering Eve: Ancient Israelite Women in Context* (New York and Oxford: Oxford University Press, 1988).

6   Phyllis Bird, *Missing Persons and Mistaken Identities: Women and Gender in Ancient Israel* (Minneapolis: Fortress Press, 1997), 28.

to be saved."[7] This kind of spiritual interpretation is common in Korean thinking.

Now we will look into an incident that shows how in these days of financial capitalism, women's bodies are a bloody battlefield of sex and money games more than ever.

The Burning Sun Club and the Capital Extracted from Women's Bodies

It all began with a cell phone in the end of 2018. The content of a group chat of fourteen, mostly entertainment stars, was shockingly exposed. It turned out that these men drugged women without their knowledge, had sex with them, taped them in secret, bragged about posting the videos, and then shared them with derogatory comments. On top of this, many other appalling crimes by the Burning Sun Club, run by one of these men, came to the fore: drugs, prostitution, embezzlement, tax evasion, illegal taping of sex videos, and the back-scratching alliance between the club and the police through bribery. We will especially focus on taking women by drugs and exploiting teens as sex workers.[8]

---

7   Jejawon, *Judges 10b-21* (Korean), (Jejawon, 1999), 657, 659.

8   "Scouters" would find runaway teen girls, often from abusive or neglectful families, and turn them over to club "MDs" (merchandisers). Then MDs acted as pimps. An undercover writer and pastor, Wongyu Ju, saw that even a sixth-grade girl was compelled to work in this way. See http://www.inews24.com/view/1165874 (accessed on Oct. 31, 2019). Although sex trafficking is illegal in Korea, the sex industry is booming through various online and off-line channels. Korea has the world's sixth-largest sex trafficking market; and, in a survey, half the men responded that they had bought sex at least once. "Where are 'men who do not buy sex'" (Korean), accessed October 31, 2019, http://www.womennews.co.kr/news/articleView.html?idxno=193325.

It was found that men secretly drugged women, whom they had only met that day, by putting GHB or other drugs in their drinks. These women were raped and sometimes secretly taped. At the club the use of drugs and sexual violence against women were pervasive; but when trouble was reported to the police, the police came to protect the club, not the victims. E-Loom, a human rights group against prostitution, said, "Gendered drugs in gendered clubs render women things and helpless."[9]

Sex workers borrow the initial capital for such things as housing, plastic surgery, cosmetics, and clothes from the pimps or banks at a very high interest rate. These workers have to pay a certain amount of money every day and a late payment, even if they are late by one day. This means that they are quickly in debt, so the repayment is impossible. One woman owed the equivalent of $1.5 million after only fourteen months. When the women are turned over to new pimps, their debts go with them. While the woman's income might be high (several tens of thousands of dollars a month), it is impossible for them to pay off the debts. Juhee Kim, a scholar in women's studies, pinpoints the irony that while sex trafficking is illegal, it is legal for financial circles to lend money to sex industry workers and get exorbitant interest.[10] Women get loans at the bottom of the financial pyramid in the name of Lady's Loan or Women Only Loan, and with their bodies mortgaged.

---

9   In a survey done by Flaming Feminist Action, 70 percent of club goers experienced sexual molestation and sexual harassment, and 20 percent experienced GHB or Zolpidem (sleeping pill, most often used in sexual crimes) directly or indirectly, in "70% of users 'have experienced sexual violence' . . . What Happens in the Club?" March 8, 2019, https://www.hankookilbo.com/News/Read/201903071742020324.

10 Juhee Kim, "Financialization of Daily Reproduction and the Extension of Freedom of Prostitutes (Korean)," *Women's Studies Review* 32.2 (2015): 29-60.

The women's group E-Loom states that the capital extracted from women's bodies ties together the drug business, sex trafficking, the medical and beauty industries, financial capital, police, the justice system, and borough offices.

On one hand, in 2018 the #MeToo movement erupted, beginning with a report of a courageous woman prosecutor, and Korean society saw a possibility of being a mature culture and going beyond a culture where sexual discrimination and violence are commonplace. On the other hand, commercialization of women's sexuality takes extreme forms in the subculture. As long as the view of women does not change, cases like the Burning Sun Club in which women are drugged and exploited will continue to happen.

Conclusion: Deconstructing the Stories

Interestingly, our ancient and modern stories seem to contain self-condemnation, undo anxiety, and judgment. "The Fairy and the Woodcutter" as oral literature has several major versions and one with a longer ending that conveys this survival anxiety and judgment.

> As time went by, the woodcutter began to worry about his mother, whom he had left behind on earth. The wife, who understood the woodcutter's feelings, provided him with a winged horse that would safely take him down to earth and back. The wife also warned the woodcutter never to get off the horse at any point. During the trip, however, the woodcutter spilled his mother's hot porridge on the horse's back, and as the startled horse reared up on its legs, he was knocked off its back. The winged horse flew back to the heavens, leaving the helpless woodcutter behind. The woodcutter was

never to return to the heavens again. Sad and alone, he later turned into a rooster that crows its grief to the skies.

This ending is not a happy one for the woodcutter. Probably women storytellers dissatisfied with the wrongs done against the woman character added the longer ending, a punishment for the woodcutter. He is not to enjoy the heavenly life.

The story of women's collective abduction in Judges 21 also seems to deconstruct itself.[11] The project to revive the Benjaminites is filled with distortion, illogic, and self-centered interpretation. The oath claimed to be made at Mizpah, "No one of us shall give his daughter in marriage to Benjamin" (21:1), does not appear in chapter 20. The mention of the oath serves as rationale to attack Jabesh-gilead and take women from there. While the Israelites seem to base their decision on the principle that all should be utterly destroyed, "including the women and the little ones" (v. 10), they violate it by saving four hundred women "who had never slept with a man" (v. 12). In the case of the abduction of women at Shiloh, the leaders prepare an absurd excuse for the "fathers and brothers" of the women taken: "We did not capture in battle a wife for each man. But neither did you incur guilt by giving your daughters to them" (v. 22). Another element that taunts the leaders is revealed when they ridiculously blame the Lord for the near extinction of the Benjaminites, the result of their own war (v. 15). The story of a battle, killing of innocent people, and sexual and other violence against women in Judges 21 contains survival anxiety and judgment.

---

11 Elsewhere I interpreted Judges 21 as the narrator's parody criticizing the gang rape of the Levite's wife and the following war. Yani Yoo, "Reading Judges 21 as a Parody: Remembering the Daughters of Jabesh-gilead and Shiloh (Korean)," in *Sexual Violence, the Bible and the Korean Church*, 90-116.

The case of the Burning Sun Club is no exception. In the conversations in their cell phone messenger program, one said, "I had it [sex] at a shopping mall. I am garbage." The other said, "That's strong. Acknowledged." The third said, "Not a murder though, but deserve to be arrested." They judged themselves as garbage and murderer-like. They knew how terrible their behavior was, revealing anxiety and judgment. A victim girl/sex worker during a phone interview with BBC answered the question of what she would like to see happen to those involved in the scandal. She said, "I hope they all die."[12]

Whether in ancient or modern times, women's time, brains, labor, bodies, and sexuality—basically, everything she has—can be bought. Some men who lack money, power, and the ability to persuade women but still want to possess them use deceit, coercion, and crime. In today's capitalist Korea, the ways to extract capital from women's bodies may appear more skillful or technologically advanced, but they are no better than the raw taking of women in Judges 21 and "The Fairy and the Woodcutter."

Taking women by deceit or violence and extracting capital from women's bodies happens everywhere. How can we change this reality? Preachers too often interpret the horrible story like Judges 21 spiritually. What can help them see that these stories vividly describe the horror of abduction, rape, and exploitation of women sexually and economically? The Church needs to deal with stories of sexual and economic exploitation critically in the Bible and the world and thereby contribute to transformation. Can the Church renew itself and the world to the extent that modern fairies would not want to go back to the heavens?

---

12 Laura Bicker, "Gangnam: The scandal rocking the playground of K-pop," *BBC News*, June 25, 2019, https://www.bbc.com/news /world-asia-48702763.

NINE

Token Racial-Ethnic Women

Living in a Juxtaposition of
Race, Gender, and Class in
Academia and the Church

HiRho Y. Park, PhD

The following quote from the book *Presumed Incompetent* points out how covert racism permeates academia and the Church:

> In an environment where great lip service is given to diversity and federal affirmative-action policies apply, overt racism is discouraged. Therefore, battles over racial and gender hierarchy are fought through individual women's bodies and minds.[1]

Universities, theological schools, and the Church acknowledge that discrimination is wrong in theory, yet their practices of discrimination perpetuate through "institutional tokenism"—a new, systemic covert racism. I am a transnational and transcultural

---

1 Gabriella Gutiérrez y Muhs et al., eds., *Presumed Incompetent* (Boulder, CO: Utah State University Press, 2012), 10.

Asian-American woman who is writing this chapter based on my own experiences from the context of being a token in academia and the Church. In the chapter I also argue that tokenism is communal; therefore, I analyze tokenism from an institutional perspective. Tokenism operates systemically under the disguise of an egalitarian vision within an organization. Therefore, tokenism should be considered an aspect of prejudice and discrimination that stem from value systems. These are my primary questions: "How does tokenism creep into women of color scholars and Church leaders as a systemic force?"; "How does institutional tokenism impact the lives of token racial-ethnic women scholars and Church leaders?"; and "What can be done?"

In 2010 the General Board of Higher Education and Ministry conducted a salary study of The United Methodist Church, which was a historical study on the status of the salary of United Methodist (UM) clergy in the U.S. The result of the survey confirmed what nobody in the denomination wanted to admit: stratification existed among the clergy. According to the study, racial-ethnic clergy received 9–15 percent less than white clergy, and clergywomen earned 13 percent less than male clergy,[2] with a racial-ethnic clergywoman at the bottom of the totem pole. In essence her salary level exposed an acute example of what it means to live in the intersection of race, gender, and class in the U.S., even within a Christian denomination. Similarly, white, non-Hispanic women made seventy-seven cents for every dollar paid to white, non-Hispanic men in 2010 in the U.S. Nine years later, in 2019, white, non-Hispanic women made seventy-nine

---

2   HeeAn Choi and Eric Johnson, "Salaries for United Methodist Clergy in the US Context," The General Board of Higher Education and Ministry, November 2010.

cents to men's one dollar.[3] The gender wage gap by race and ethnicity in the U.S. as of 2019 revealed that Latinas, Native American women, African-American women, and Asian women make fifty-four to ninety cents for every dollar paid to white, non-Hispanic men.[4]

According to the "Women in Leadership" study from the Association of Theological Schools (ATS), the representation of women in executive leadership positions, such as CEO and CAO, in theological schools for the last twenty years has not exceeded 30 percent. The report used numbers, not ratio, since the number of racial-ethnic women representation was too slim; for example, women CEOs who are of African descent grew from 2 percent to 5 percent; Asian descent stayed at 1 percent; and Latina descent rose from basically nonexistent to 1 percent, from 2009 to 2018.[5] This data is evidence that the demographics of higher-education institutions and the Church are still very white, male-dominated, and culturally Western-oriented. There could be many contributing factors to the slow progress of the inclusion of women, especially racial-ethnic women. However, I want to argue that institutional tokenism is one of the critical barriers

---

3   "The Wage Gap Over Time: In Real Dollars, Women See a Continuing Gap," National Committee on Pay Equity, October 2019, https://www.pay-equity.org/info-time.html.

4   "Quantifying America's Gender Wage Gap by Race/Ethnicity," National Partnership for Women & Families, March 2020, https://www.nationalpartnership.org/our-work/resources/economic-justice/fair-pay/quantifying-americas-gender-wage-gap.pdf.

5   Deborah H. C. Gin, "Women in Leadership survey: what we found may not be what you think," *Colloquy Online*, The Association of Theological Schools (June 2018) https://www.ats.edu/uploads/resources/publications-presentations/colloquy-online/women-in-leadership-survey.pdf.

against the full inclusion of racial-ethnic women in academic and Church leadership.

Living at the Intersection of Race, Gender, and Class

Angela P. Harris and Carmen G. González say that for a racial-ethnic woman to be in higher education for the sake of diversity is a good starting point. However, it comes with such a high cost of her physical and psychological well-being, balance, and confidence.[6] This ambiguous position—being a token—applies to the Church also. The Church may preach the liberating power of Jesus Christ for all, yet not to the extent that liberation includes racial-ethnic people, especially women, in positions of senior leadership. Major denominational theological schools may teach inclusiveness in a classroom; however, its lived theology—real theology—feeds the power of Western, male-oriented perspectives. According to James West, an economics professor at Baylor University, creating a chief diversity officer in an ivory tower does not help diversify faculty demographics. Instead, diversity of tenured faculty tended to decrease in many universities after schools created a chief diversity officer.[7] What does this mean? My interpretation is that a cognitive understanding of inclusiveness, unfortunately, gave birth to tokenism in practice.

---

6   Muhs et al., *Presumed Incompetent*, 1-7.

7   Clare Hansen, "Do Chief Diversity Officers Help Diversify a University's Faculty? This Study Found No Evidence," The Chronicle of Higher Education, September 6, 2018, https://www.chronicle.com/article /Do-Chief-Diversity-Officers/244460. West and his colleagues analyzed the faculty diversity of 462 research institutions in United States before and after they hired chief diversity officers.

I. How does tokenism creep into women of color scholars and Church leaders as a systemic force?

What Is Tokenism?

Rosabeth Moss Kanter, a sociologist and professor at Harvard Business School, conducted a pioneering study on tokenism in 1977. She defined tokenism from a numerical analysis. Tokenism happens when the ratio of the number of dominants to others is 85:15 or less. A token could be the only one or two in the context.[8] As an Asian-American woman, I have been the only Asian and woman in many academic, business, and Church settings.

Tokenism is a result of "aversive racism,"[9] which represents hypocritical behavior that promotes an egalitarian value on the surface yet practices race- and gender-biased behaviors behind the scenes. In my experience, aversive racism exists at the highest levels of academia and the Church, regrettably. Tokenism represents a guilt-driven placebo and is the product of a fear-centered value system. It happens when those who are dominant, in terms of power and numbers, interact with people who are different than the majority in the institution. For example, those who are educated want to believe in egalitarian diversity and understand what the right thing to do is intellectually. Yet it seems that practicing egalitarianism on a regular basis is a different matter.

---

8   Rosabeth Moss Kanter, "Some Effects of Proportions on Group Life: Skewed Sex Ratios and Responses to Token Women," *American Journal of Sociology* 82, no. 5 (1977): 966.

9   Yolanda Flores Niemann, "The Making of a Token: A Case Study of Stereotype Threat, Stigma, Racism, and Tokenism in Academe," *Frontiers: A Journal of Women Studies* 20, no. 1 (1999): 120.

What Are the Symptoms of Tokenism?

Rosabeth Moss Kanter analyzed tokenism within corporate America using three words: visibility, polarization, and assimilation.[10] Visibility heightens performance pressure. For example, token racial-ethnic women have to work harder than their colleagues to have their achievement noticed, since their racial-ethnic and gender status overshadows their performance at all times; they are considered mere embellishments of an institution and offered as evidence of racial-ethnic and gender inclusion.

Polarization of differences exacerbates vulnerabilities and the exclusion of tokens. Yolanda Niemann called "simultaneously, perverse visibility and convenient invisibility" a "double-edged sword."[11] Polarization often results in token racial-ethnic women being visible during public meetings yet excluded in informal gatherings.[12] In my own experience I was physically visible as the only Asian woman in the institution, yet invisible as a scholar/leader at the same institution, excluded from the critical decision-making process despite my education and credentials. Only rarely was I invited to private gatherings during my tenure at the organization.

Role strain or "role encapsulation"[13] is indicative of the pressure to assimilate to dominant leadership values. A propensity toward assimilation results in the entrapment of token racial-ethnic women; they try to simultaneously meet the expectations of the organization and represent their racial-ethnic community,

---

10 Kanter, "Some Effects," 971.

11 Niemann, "The Making of a Token," 111.

12 Niemann, 199.

13 Janice D. Yoder, "Rethinking Tokenism: Looking beyond Numbers," *Gender and Society* 5, no. 2 (1991): 178.

all the while confronting gender-stereotype role assumptions. Gabriella Gutiérrez y Muhs and Yolanda Niemann both talk about the heavy workload and role strain placed on racial-ethnic women in the workplace. Token racial-ethnic women seek to excel as scholars and leaders, and they also understand that they should represent their racial-ethnic community for the institution's diversity agenda. This imposed burden is called "cultural taxation."[14] For example, I was the only director responsible for five different areas, including women and racial-ethnic issues, while other directors focused on only one or two areas.

Manifestation of Tokenism Institutions

The underlying force of racial-ethnic tokenism is the stigma of incompetence, especially with women. A token slowly starts questioning her self-efficacy, questioning whether she was hired as a scholar, a leader, or simply a racial-ethnic representative. Niemann calls this a "forced duality,"[15] and a token feels that she has to choose between being competent and being only a statistic—a racial-ethnic woman. Eventually, she often falls into undermining her own competence with self-defeating behaviors. A token racial-ethnic woman often is overqualified for her job compared to her colleagues; however, her ideas and work need the approval of those who are dominant, which involves silence and submission. For example, her ideas do not go far unless supported by white colleagues.

---

14 Dave A. Louis et al., "Listening to Our Voices: Experiences of Black Faculty at Predominantly White Research Universities with Microaggression," *Journal of Black Studies* 47, no. 5 (2016): 457.
15 Niemann, "The Making of a Token," 117.

Institutional Microaggressions

Robert House asserts that "leadership is culturally contingent."[16] Powerful cultural forces influence our leadership, and we evaluate leadership based on our cultural norms and values. Therefore, if a token's leadership style is not familiar to the dominant, there are "subtle and blatant attempts at punishing the unexpected behavior."[17] The punishment happens in a systemic way, mostly as institutional microaggression—"a form of systemic, everyday racism used to keep those at the racial margins in their place."[18] Acts of institutional microaggression are "invisible social ill[s]"[19] and usually unconscious forms of intimidation and hostile force directed toward the token. This research also validates my experience of institutional microaggressions, which are subtle and insidious and which often left me puzzled and powerless to respond. Institutional microaggressions manifested as belittling ("You are just a perfectionist"); sabotaging (giving lip service to a project but not supporting it when budgets go up for approval); and stereotyping (discrediting and denigrating comments based solely on gender, race, or social location, such as "Can I talk to the pastor?" or "Can I talk to the dean?" when you are the person in charge).

II. How does institutional tokenism impact the lives of token racial-ethnic women scholars and Church leaders?

---

16 Robert J. House et al., eds., *Culture, Leadership, and Organizations: The GLOBE Study of 62 Societies* (Thousand Oaks, CA: SAGE Publications, 2004), 5.

17 Muhs et al., *Presumed Incompetent*, 3.

18 Louis et al., "Listening to Our Voices," 455.

19 Louis et al., 454.

Token racial-ethnic women experience institutional microaggressions in these categories:

Quarantine and Dissension among Tokens

Ironically, a racial-ethnic woman is hired under the banner of inclusion. Yet, a token is further isolated if she is deemed successful and exceeds the institution's expectations. Punishment comes if a token shows to be a strong woman who insists on full rights within an organization and displays competence; she may be considered as dangerous from a political perspective of the institution. The punishment is exclusion by isolating an individual from higher-level decision-making processes, therefore depriving the token of pertinent information to succeed. Rosabeth Moss Kanter calls this "quarantine,"[20] which means excluding tokens from salient opportunities, discussions, and informal socialization. For example, through the grapevine a racial-ethnic woman token may hear about perks that other staff enjoy after a few years into the job, rather than learning about them during the hiring process. Let's think about another example of being a racial-ethnic clergywoman in a local church. A church is a place where relationship-building and informal interaction is key to being a successful leader. However, a token is set up for failure because of "quarantine," which happens, even perhaps unwittingly, by members of the congregation.[21]

An unfortunate and evil side of tokenism can be the desire of tokens to collude with the dominants, which can set tokens against one another. Gabriella Gutiérrez y Muhs argues that "academic institutions may pit faculty of color against one

---

20 Kanter, "Some Effects," 978.
21 Kanter, 987.

another by bestowing lavish rewards on one faculty member to avoid accusations of racism when they denigrate another."[22] The institutional tokenism that sets tokens against each other happens not only from a racial perspective but also among women. The tragedy is that those who receive favor from the dominants fall into arrogance, perhaps not knowing that he or she is also a victim of the same tokenism.

Unequal Opportunities

One of the main reasons for publishing this book is to provide a venue to hear the voices of African and Asian women's theological scholarship. It is challenging for racial-ethnic women to obtain an opportunity to publish their academic work. It is a known fact that token racial-ethnic women are usually placed in positions deemed to be more practical and of lesser value. For example, many women of color are placed in the area of administrative faculty or clinical faculty. For the token racial-ethnic woman, institutional distrust is embedded in her existence; however, she may not understand that there is a glass ceiling of institutional advancement. Despite this, she struggles against the invisible ceiling constructed of racism, sexism, classism, and stigmatism in her pursuit of promotion. Eventually, she runs the significant risk of being suffocated by institutional microaggressions, often berating herself with demoralizing thoughts and self-dismissal. Self-blaming is a feeling of inferiority and illegitimacy and not uncommon, even though a token is usually overqualified for her job. Self-doubt and self-condescension are results of stigmatization and institutional tokenism.

---

22 Muhs et al., *Presumed Incompetent*, 11.

Stigmatization and Entrapment

Lorrain Code asserts that "tokenism has been used by dominant social and political groups to reinforce individualistic interpretations of its significance."[23] The danger of institutional tokenism is that both the token and institution are not striving to be the best they can be from the very beginning. It is because an individual is placed within an "anti-affirmative action sentiment"[24] in an institution, and the institution evaluates her from a distorted lens, that of incompetence, a label that comes from being viewed as a woman of color.

The token is placed in a no-win situation from the beginning. For example, Asian Americans are considered "perpetual foreigners," permanent followers and learners in the U.S., according to Frank H. Wu.[25] They are often treated as if they are not fully mature adults; a few aspects may contribute to that: language, stature, and looking younger than their age. Even though the institutions that practice tokenism may behave as if they are on the frontline of inclusion, there is the unconscious basis of expecting a token to be a follower on all levels. The institution also expects the stereotypical gender role of submission if you are a token racial-ethnic woman.

Another reality of women of color tokens in a white majority institution is juggling the dynamics of fear of retaliation, risk of speaking up, fighting against dismissal, and being silenced. Paradoxically, tokens are expected to perform exceptionally; yet

---

23 Lorraine Code, "Tokenism," in *Feminist Research: Prospect and Retrospect*, ed. Tancred-sheriff Peta (Montreal: McGill-Queen's University Press, 1988), 246-54.

24 Niemann, "The Making of a Token," 113.

25 Frank H. Wu, *Yellow: Race in America Beyond Black and White* (New York: Basic Books, 2002), 79-130.

if they outperform the dominant as to humiliate them, tokens will experience retaliation.[26] Retaliation comes in various forms, such as sexual harassment, undue scrutiny of work performance, wage inequalities, and limited opportunities for promotion. If a token protests by speaking up, what is perceived as too often, there is punishment, as we have seen above. This is because a token is considered as "a mascot, cheerleader, or seductress,"[27] rather than a serious intellectual or leader. As we discussed earlier, women of color tokens are trapped by the demand of visibility, representation of their master status (race, ethnicity, gender, culture, sexuality, etc.), and the pressure to remain invisible (even if they are competent on the job) so that the dominant will not be threatened. The above dynamics explain the reason why bright racial-ethnic women are usually in a lower rank of the power hierarchy.

III. What can be done?

Tokenism operates from within an institution yet targets individuals and demoralizes bright persons who happen to be part of a racial-ethnic minority. As such, tokenism is more devious than overt racism, as the entire system can be levied against one individual to "keep her in her place." I have noticed that higher-education institutions and the Church both approach inclusiveness with varying degrees of intellectual and spiritual romanticism, which can result in tokenism. The point is that institutional tokenism will leave scars on both the institution and the individual, preventing all of us from advancing with creativity and diverse leadership, both of which are drivers for institutional success.

One way to address tokenism is through coaching, with token racial-ethnic women coaching other token racial-ethnic women.

---

26 Kanter, "Some Effects," 974.
27 Muhs et al., *Presumed Incompetent*, 3.

It has been proved that those who are under constant microaggressions can develop "higher levels of hypertension, cardiovascular disease, and coronary heart disease."[28] Consequently, women of color in academia and the Church must seek to build a network of support among each other. Building a supportive network could be done by mentoring, coaching, and befriending one another.

According to J. Val Hastings, "At its core, coaching is about empowering others."[29] Coaching seeks to empower others by asking powerful questions. The goal of the process is to bring out the best in a person. The foundation of coaching is the belief that listening is the beginning of healing and points us to discover anew. In a case of women of color who have been scarred by institutional tokenism, healing begins when someone validates the experience of disapproval, disparaging remarks, and devaluing her existence by listening to her without judgment. Even though a coach can coach anybody using powerful questions, coaching is contextual also. Token racial-ethnic women in theological schools and the Church can listen to one another deeply since they understand institutional exploitation, marginalization, powerlessness, cultural imperialism, systemic violence, silencing, deprecation, and vilification.[30]

For the longest time I could not see any positive aspect of being a token in an institution as a racial-ethnic woman scholar and leader. However, I am convinced that if token racial-ethnic

---

28 Muhs et al., 7.

29 J. Val Hastings, *Ministry 3.0: How Today's Church Leaders Are Using Coaching to Transform Ministry* (St. Peters, MO: Cathedral Rose Books, 2012), loc. 126 of 2333, Kindle ed.

30 Elisabeth Schüssler Fiorenza, *Wisdom Ways: Introducing Feminist Biblical Interpretation* (Maryknoll, NY: Orbis Books, 2001), 109-10.

women work together by building a supportive network, we will make a path of transformation rather than remaining victims of institutional microaggressions. By coaching one another we can change a course of institutional tokenism so that an institution that hires a token will be a place for racial-ethnic women's empowerment. After all, institutional tokenism impacts an individual in the most elusive but insidious ways. It is better to combat it as a community of powerful token racial-ethnic women rather than remain depreciated individuals by academia and the Church. Living in a juxtaposition of race, gender, and class is a sacred calling from God to advance human society with equity and inclusivity. When a token racial-ethnic woman is aware of her calling, she will be able to claim her God-given scholarship and leadership with strength, courage, and determination. Her prophetic role will transform our higher-education and religious institutions slowly but surely.

About the Contributors

Djessou Epse Atsin Djoman Brigitte, PhD is a pastor in The United Methodist Church in Côte d'Ivoire and assistant professor of theology at Institut Superieur de Theologie D'Abadjin-Doume (Istha, Abidjan, Côte d'Ivoire) and Protestant University of Central Africa (Puca, Yaounde, Cameroon). She is also a pastor of The United Methodist Church Côte d'Ivoire; member of Texts Committee in the United Methodist Church Côte d'Ivoire; member of the Legal Committee in the United Methodist Church Côte d'Ivoire; member of the Circle of African Clergy Women and Theologians Engaged; and member of African Clergy Women's Association of The United Methodist Church.

Memory Chikosi, MA is a publisher, an ordained pastor-lecturer, and a chaplain at United Theological College (UTC) in Harare, Zimbabwe; and associate chairperson of the Zimbabwe West Annual Conference of The United Methodist Board of Education and Ministry. She holds a diploma in theology obtained at UTC in Zimbabwe, a diploma in religious studies earned at University of Zimbabwe, and a master's degree in theological studies attained at Boston University. Chikosi served six local churches before she started teaching at UTC.

Elaine Wei-Fun Goh, ThD (SEAGST/ATESEA Theological Union) is dean of studies and lecturer in Old Testament studies at the Seminari Theoloji Malaysia in Seremban, Negeri Sembilan, Malaysia. She is the author of *Cross-Textual Reading of Ecclesiastes with the Analects: In Search of Political Wisdom in a Disordered World.* Her published articles include "An Intertextual Reading of Ruth and Proverbs 31:10-31 with a Chinese Woman's perspective," in *Reading Ruth in Asia*, edited by Jione Heava and Peter H. W. Lau (2015), pages 73–87. Her recent works in Mandarin include *Biblical Interpretation: How to Study the Old Testament and the New Testament* (2017); and *Rediscovering the Bible: Book of Ecclesiastes* (2019).

Helena Angelica Gustavo Guidione, BD teaches at Cambine Theological Seminary in Inhambane Province, Mozambique. She is married to Dinis Armando Guidione and has a beautiful seven-year-old daughter. She studied at Ricatla Theological Seminary in Maputo, Mozambique from 2003 to 2006 and at Africa University in Zimbabwe, where she received a bachelor's of divinity degree. She has been a pastor in the Furvela parish Nazareth parishes.

Cynthia A. Bond Hopson, PhD is assistant general secretary, The Black College Fund and Ethnic Concerns, General Board of Higher Education and Ministry, The United Methodist Church. She earned her BA in mass communications from Clark College (now Clark Atlanta University), her MS in journalism from Murray

State University, and her PhD in journalism from Southern Illinois University, Carbondale. In 2017 she received a doctor of humane letters degree from the historic Bethune-Cookman University, and in 2019 the Thurston Group of Washington State awarded her a lifetime achievement award for her commitment to higher education. She has been a tenured member of the journalism faculty at the University of Memphis and has taught at Murray State University and Lane College.

Hyun Ju Lee, PhD is associate professor of English at Methodist Theological University in Seoul, Korea. She studied medieval English literature and received her PhD at Ewha Women's University in Seoul, Korea. She also has her DMin from Wesley Theological Seminary in Washington, DC. She studied TESOL (Teaching English to Speakers of Other Languages) at Teachers College, Columbia University in New York. Lee has translated nine books including *Le Morte D'arthur (1469-70?)* sponsored by the National Research Foundation of Korea. In addition Lee has written ten books related to her studies, such as *The Poetry and Devotion of Western Protestant Missionaries in the Beginning of the Twentieth Century in Korea* (2008) and *We Want to Be Real Christians I & II* (published by Korean Methodist Church in 2013). Her English grammar book, *My First English Diary* (2002), which is also translated in Chinese, is still on the bookshelves in Korean bookstores. Most recently she published the book *"Jesu Is My Soul of Music": Studies on Charles Wesley's Hymns* (2018).

Quynh-Hoa Nguyen, PhD (PhD, Religion, Claremont Graduate University; MDiv, Claremont School of Theology) is a missionary with the Global Ministries of The United Methodist Church, serving as director of leadership development in Vietnam. Committed to the theological education of the Vietnamese pastors and laity, she has special responsibilities in developing pastoral and lay leadership as well as local trainers through teaching at Wesley Theological College. Her research interests include the Bible and marginalized peoples, Vietnamese social-cultural engagement of biblical texts, Christian identities, Vietnamese Christianity and society, and ethnography.

HiRho Y. Park, PhD is vice president for International Relations and Advancement at Huree University in Ulaanbaatar, Mongolia. Park formerly directed professional development including digital education, especially for clergywomen and racial-ethnic clergy at the General Board of Higher Education and Ministry of the UMC, for fifteen years. Park is an author of *Christian Spiritual Coaching and Wesleyan Quadrilateral* (2017) and *Develop Intercultural Competence* (2019). Park is a co-editor *of Breaking through the Stained Glass Ceiling* (2013), a contributor to *Encyclopedia of Christian Education* (2015) and *The Upper Room Disciplines 2019,* and a co-general editor of *Nevertheless She Leads: Postcolonial Women's Leadership in the Church* (2020) with M. Kathryn Armistead. She also published *Wesleyan Ecclesiology in a Global Context* (2011) and *Creating Christian Community Through the Cross-Racial Appointment* (2000).

Yani Yoo, PhD (Union Theological Seminary, New York) is a visiting professor at Methodist Theological University in Seoul, Korea. She has published many articles including "Desiring the Empire: Reading the Book of Esther in Twenty-first Century Korea," in *Migration and Diaspora: Exegetical Voices of Women in Northeast Asian Countries* (2014) and "Women's Leadership Fragmented: Examples in the Bible and the Korean Church," in *Korean Feminists in Conversation with the Bible, Church and Society* (2011). She is also the author of *God of Abraham, Rebekah, and Jacob* (Korean, 2009) and *From Eve to Esther: Her in the Bible* (Korean, 2014).